A GOODLY HERITAGE

A
GOODLY
HERITAGE

BY
MARY ELLEN CHASE

WITH ILLUSTRATIONS BY
MAITLAND DE GOGORZA

NEW YORK
HENRY HOLT AND COMPANY

To

ELEANOR SHIPLEY DUCKETT

Est enim amicitia nihil aliud nisi omnium divinarum humanarumque rerum cum benevolentia et caritate consensio, qua quidem haud scio an excepta sapientia nil quicquam melius homini sit a dis immortalibus datum.

CICERO.

The lines are fallen unto me in pleasant places; yea, I have a goodly heritage.

Psalm 16:6.

CONTENTS

CONTENTS

A GOODLY HERITAGE

PROLOGUE

"I HOPE my readers will not think me vain for writing my life," wrote the "fantastical, original-brained" Margaret Cavendish, Duchess of Newcastle in 1655 while she was still in her early thirties, "since there have been many that have done the like, as Cesar, Ovid, and many more, both men and women, and I know no reason I may not do it as well as they: but I verily believe some censuring Readers will scornfully say, why hath this Lady writ her own Life? since none cares to know whose daughter she was or whose wife she is, or how she was bred, or what fortunes she had, or how she lived, or what humour or disposition she was of? I answer that it is true, that 'tis to no purpose to the Readers, but it is to the Authoress, because I write it for my own sake, not theirs."

It is safe to say that not a little of the independence of "Mad Madge of Newcastle" solaces the spirits and guides the hands of us who would write of our own humours and fortunes. We, too, fear censuring and scornful Readers, if perchance any readers at all fall to our portion. Yet if there be aught of truth in the Epicurean doctrine of life as the goal of life, if experience itself and not its fruits is the de-

3

sire and the end of a sojourn here, then it is at least not inconceivable that there should be those of us who, first of all for our own sakes, wish to recount those past experiences and to record those past impressions which dictate alike our present and our future. We are further urged onward, once our own self-indulgence is assured, by the importunings of our subjects. Like the "certain dank gardens" in Stevenson's essay which "cry aloud for a murder," so these circumstances and incidents, places and persons which have made us what we are for better or for worse—static or progressive, grave or gay, orthodox or iconoclastic, past or future-minded, æsthetic or utilitarian—command their just due of narration and of description.

The convincing, yea, the entertaining chronicler of the past must be neither a sentimentalist nor yet a dogmatist. For such a pleasant task humour and insight are surely more reliable retainers than admiration and self-pity; and only the best minds of a far-distant future can adjudge one era as better than another. It is well, too, as Edmund Gosse suggests in the Preface to his admirable *Father and Son,* if such a chronicler be relatively young. Though promised as a boon by the prophet, the dreams of the old are treacherous assistants to the social historian, whose memory must be clear and vivid and whose estimation of values must be neither enhanced nor dimmed by the passing of many years.

Like Margaret Cavendish, therefore, who, con-

tinuing her madness, published at the age of forty-
three her life of the "thrice Noble, High, and Puis-
sant" Duke, her husband, and doubtless as "ridicu-
lous," as Pepys and others of that century found her,
in any thought that these records of a past age may
be of interest and worth except to myself and those
immediately connected with me, I begin at the same
age to write of Maine seacoast life and influences as
I knew them in the twenty-five or thirty years preceding the Great War. I write like her, largely for
my own sake, partly in gratitude to the gods who
set me in such pleasant places and gave me such a
goodly heritage, and partly in the hope that these
accurate sketches of New England people and places,
religion, industry, and education may prove of interest to readers of like tradition and experience.

For we live, indeed, in a New World. By the invention and perfection of manifold engines, which
have revolutionized transportation alike on land and
on sea, by the mechanization and consequent spread
of industry, by the inevitable internationalism of
outlook which has followed in the wake of the Great
War, the face of American life has become as completely divorced from the period of which I write
as were the late years of the fifteenth century divorced from the former by the invention of print-
ing. The parallelism is, perhaps, not a poor one. For
as suddenly as the early presses converted an old
world into a new, so suddenly has the widespread use
of motors of every sort abandoned a relatively stable

past for a hurrying present. The young of this new age, having no perspective and believing in the only time they know, are unconscious of any revolution; the old are either sceptical and resentful, or, in some few cases, annoyed that so soon cut off they must fly away with no certain knowledge of what will happen next. But the middle-aged, those millions among us whose years fall between thirty and seventy, these are acutely conscious of a new world for which most of them by training, environment, and education were totally unprepared. Moreover, in this mighty group are the matured and alert minds of the country, the productive scholars and teachers, parents with adolescent children, industrial leaders in the prime of contributive life. These, to a large extent formed by the past, must adjust themselves to a new present. Some accomplish this feat (for feat it is!) easily and gladly, rejoicing in the physical, intellectual, and spiritual freedom of their children and grandchildren; others, so painfully that homes are worse than divided and school and college classrooms wage an eternal war betwixt conflicting standards of value; still others, not at all, so that if lay monasteries, free of theological convictions, were devised as a refuge for ailing minds instead of for sin-sick souls, they would be filled overnight with misanthropes and misfits.

I write as one of the multitude of the middle-aged, as one who, formed by the thirty years before the War, must yet live, think, and work in the present, contributing if may be to the sum-total of the assets of a new era. What have such formative years, spent in and moulded by relatively stable influences, to contribute to a seemingly unstable present? Was the outlook of 1890, of 1900, of 1910, particularly in their social aspects, saner and more reliable than that of 1930? Time and time alone can probably answer such questions. But perhaps an honest presentation of the ideas and the ideals under which so many millions of us were reared may not come amiss. For although I write of New England life and particularly of that life as it was experienced in the State of Maine, the account cannot be termed sectional in that out of New England so many of our Western states were originally made. And of all the New England states Maine contributed a major portion. Indeed, the outstanding rural character of that northern division of Massachusetts, which became a state only in 1820, together with the comparatively late development of her industries, was the cause of much migration to wider and more prosperous fields. One has but to live in the Middle and Far West to realize how great a number of western Americans were reared in transported New England homes and how many of these claimed, and still claim, allegiance to the State of Maine.

I write, then, of a scene which can rightly be termed a native American one, and I write not to draw a moral but to paint a picture. Rather would I seize upon what made an age distinctive than attempt

to present that age as a palliative or as an example
to a different present. Nor do I portray exceptional
circumstances or an exceptional environment. The
conditions under which I was reared, my family and
its fortunes, my education, my religious training, I
believe to have been as nearly typical as it is possible
to find among our native American stock. Nor is my
purpose an overly zealous one. I write alike of the
comic and serious aspects of adolescence under a waning yet still vigorous Puritanism; of the lively effects
of the seafaring tradition; of education before it became an "experiment." I shall be satisfied if these
records of a past, near and yet by the force of circumstances immeasurably far removed, may serve to
entertain those to whom that past is still memorable,
may serve to amuse and to surprise those who will
never know it.

Smith College,
Northampton, Massachusetts,
January, 1932.

PART I

SOCIAL BACKGROUND AND AMENITIES

CHAPTER I

ENVIRONMENT AND HERITAGE

THE coast of Maine, which hurls its rockstrewn headlands for twenty-five hundred miles from Kittery Point to Eastport, boasts no lovelier section than that contained between Frenchman's and Penobscot Bays. Here the country is at once more compact and more varied with small, unproductive fields sloping seaward and rolling, wooded hills stretching backward and upward until they are lost in an uneven black skyline of pines and firs. Innumerable islands of every conceivable shape and size rise from the depths of a less tumultuous ocean than that which thunders against the red cliffs of Mount Desert; and although the rough and scanty beaches offer no warm stretches of sand like those at Old Orchard and Kennebunk, the land is less rigorous of contour and more friendly than those great, tumbling reaches which embrace Penobscot Bay and receive its river.

It is a section of small valleys and, therefore, of streams rather than of rivers—streams whose widening mouths receive twice daily the incoming tide to cover their rocks and ledges and to silence their turbulence. The promontories, extending seaward, embrace of necessity smaller bodies of water, coves in

11

comparison with the great bays west and east—Casco, Penobscot, Frenchman's, Passamaquoddy, and Fundy. Yet Blue Hill Bay, though less wide and deep than its neighbours, is no cove to those who, sailing its waters, look northward where at its extreme head rises the great hill, a landmark to mariners past and present and a suggestion to more travelled eyes of Vesuvius beyond the Bay of Naples.

Doubtless the contours of this more deeply indented coast and the character of the land itself explain its late exploration and settlement. Of those early voyagers who may have sailed from Fundy to Casco—Cabot, Hawkins, Gosnold, Martin Pring, Sieur de Monts, Champlain, Weymouth, Rosier, Captain John Smith—we cannot be certain that one of them left the wider, safer courses of the outer ocean to cruise within the narrower confines of Blue Hill Bay itself. But just as certainly surmise is open to all lovers of that desultory occupation. And one is quite free to imagine that Champlain, who in September of 1604 cruised from Passamaquoddy to Penobscot Bay and River, could not have found, even in his energetic nature, sufficient strength to resist a nearer sight of that hill, which crowns the bay, once he had seen in the autumn haze its purple symmetry from the waters beyond Mount Desert. That he makes in his *Journal* no mention of such an exciting detour may be explained on the ground of the sheer inadequacy of words!

The earliest settlers of the Maine coast, whether

Royalists and Anglicans from Virginia and the mother country or Puritans from Massachusetts Bay, were not enticed by these shallower coves, by these rockier hills and valleys. Far more tempting were the navigable waters of the Kennebec and the Penobscot, the good harbour of old Falmouth, now Portland. Success in fishing required a nearer proximity to deeper ocean, in ship-building and launching, a like nearness to necessary supplies. One hundred years before the sheltered coves of Blue Hill Bay were dotted with their first log-cabins, Passamaquoddy and Frenchman's had seen the rise and fall of Jesuit missions, the flourishing and waning of French trading stations; Penobscot had known the fast-succeeding rivalries of French, Dutch, and English; Casco had echoed to the sounds of the mallet and the hammer and of the launching of full-rigged ships.

Doubtless, too, the comparative isolation of the land bordering the inner arms of Blue Hill Bay dictated the character of its first settlers. They were men of small means, of shrewdness and of enterprise rather than of large ambitions. In a petition sent in January, 1762, to the General Court of Massachusetts they describe themselves as "husbandmen," living near the towns of Haverhill, Beverly, and Andover, "without lands sufficient for themselves and sons." They humbly beg, therefore, for a "considerable Tract of Unappropriated Wilderness Land and Islands," as they shall find suitable, "in some place or places on the Sea Coast between Passamaquoddy Bay and the land near the Penobscot." Their petition, granted two months later in the House of Representatives, was delayed until such time as "His Majestyes Royal Approbation" might be obtained. Whereupon two of the petitioners, Joseph Wood and John Roundy by name, weary of waiting and eager to trust the security of distance and inaccessibility, came without permission and with no rights whatsoever made themselves lords of a beautiful but unproductive coast.

A few years later they were followed by others of the petitioners, who, more wary than themselves, waited at least for the "Incouragement" of the Governor and Council of Massachusetts; and in less than two decades Woods, Roundys, Carletons, Parkers, Osgoods, Peterses, Candages, Holts, Hortons, and Hinckleys had not only cleared arable land, made "Rhodes," and built their homes, but had formed neighbouring settlements to which they lured other husbandmen from north of Boston. At first they named their settlement East Boston, perhaps in the hope of favour from the powers of Massachusetts Bay, but the name was soon changed to Blue Hill. Was there perhaps among their practical minds an unknown poet who would brook no other?

Farmers they were only in so far as they must of necessity feed and clothe their families. They early made use both of the streams and of the tide to turn the wheels of their small mills—mills for carding and fulling, for sawing staves and larger lumber, grist and even cotton mills. Finding the hire of vessels from larger ports too dear for the exportation of their products, they erected adequate docks and before the turn of the century were building, as well as coasting vessels, brigs and barques of respectable tons burden, which they launched from their own shores and manned with their own sons.

Probably no special endowments either of mind or of hand can be accredited to them; perhaps, indeed, they had been relatively unimportant men in the larger communities from whence they came. But the hardships and exigencies of pioneer life developed, as always, whatever initiative they had; and if we can believe the records of the town and of the outlying villages which they founded, they did not hide their small talents in the earth. As their ancestors a century earlier had found in Massachusetts no social or religious obstacles to stem their rising, so here they found no impediments which their toil could not remove, no hindrances which an older civilization might raise against their progress. Their sons became men of wider vision and of longer thoughts. Imbued by coastwise journeyings to Boston, New York, and Philadelphia with loftier seafaring ambitions, they became the lesser officers of larger vessels and in due time, as the clippers became mistresses of the seas, the masters of ships in the foreign trade. Far voyages brought in their wake farther mental horizons as well as the steady accumu-

lation, to the best of them, of means. Their grandsons built substantial homes of wood and brick,
homes with wide-mouthed chimneys, broad roofs,
and beautiful doorways; they spoke familiarly of
London and Hongkong, Calcutta and Mozambique;
in the fifties and sixties they sent their more bookish
sons to college, to Yale and Bowdoin, Harvard and
Princeton. And when the nineties came and the turn
of another century was not far distant, their great-
great-grandchildren told their children of them with
the realization that out of simple beginnings, by toil,
by adaptation to circumstances, and by seizure of occasions, one generation can give rise to a better.

For they were assuredly of average English stock.
In more than a century no "foreigner," not even a
Scotchman or an Irishman, appeared among them.
According to the terms of the grant which the Prov-
ince of Massachusetts finally accorded them, they
were "good Protestants," Congregationalists. Their
settlement, their industries, their manner of life and
thought, their religious and social background were
like those of thousands of their contemporaries in a
hundred like localities. They were, in a word, typical
of the middle class English who made New England
and who through their descendants widened her borders by the extension of her influences into other and
larger fields.

"THEIR GRANDSONS BUILT SUBSTANTIAL HOMES—WITH WIDE-MOUTHED CHIMNEYS AND BROAD ROOFS"

CHAPTER II

MY MOTHER'S FAMILY

(1)

JOSEPH WOOD, that squatter on land not his own, was my great-great-great-grandfather. The distinction, if it be a distinction, cannot be termed rare since many another through his numerous children and grand-children can claim a like honour. As in every isolated pioneer settlement, so in his. His sons and his daughters married the daughters and the sons of his neighbours, until after five generations the process of untangling the same thread, woven and interwoven through various families, is a major operation.

That my great-great-grandmother, Edith Wood, was the first white child to be born on the shores of Blue Hill Bay is likewise an honour which I must share with scores, yea, with hundreds of her descendants. Large families in eighteenth century New England were the rule, the word being interpreted rather in the nature of an unwritten law than merely of a custom. One not only contributed to the future needs of a new settlement by such production within the home, but served the Lord as well. Ten, twelve, even fifteen children excited only admiration; and parents

17

with but a paltry five or six to their credit were called into question on the grounds not only of hardihood and normality but of duty. Nevertheless, widespread as is the honour, it is yet cherished; and the name *Edith* has been handed down in many families, my mother and my sister alike still bearing it with pride.

My mother's people became early tinged with the Baptist "heresy." This defection was regarded as only slightly less sinister than that resulting from the itinerant Methodists. In the beginning of 1803 the first pastor of the first Congregational Church in Blue Hill, the Reverend Jonathan Fisher, noted in his record: "Much exertion has been made by the itinerant Methodists to introduce their peculiar tenets, much resembling those of the ancient Pelagians. Numbers have flocked after them. The pastor has felt it to be his duty to attend their meetings and publicly state what he believes to be the Truth in opposition to error disseminated. The result has been favourable beyond expectation, and the current toward the Methodists has subsided." But such good fortune did not follow the eloquence of the early Baptist preachers. On March 14, 1805, the pastor again wrote, after a peroration devoted to "this vaine and unseemly talk of immersion as necessary to salvation": "A Brother and Sister, having offered reasons, withdrew from the communion of the church. Their reasons were that they considered baptism to be the only door of admission to the church of

God and that immersion after believing is essential to baptism." One may surmise with what relief a few years later he penned this comment: "Several of those withdrawn to the Baptists have removed from the town. Two of them have been ordained as Baptist ministers, men of good character but of small education."

Of these two one was my mother's great-grandfather on the paternal side, Benjamin Lord. What manner of man he was has been lost in the indistinctness of many years. He may well have been "of small education," but assuredly he was of no small zeal in the promulgation of his new faith. Upon his removal from the settlement at Blue Hill, which removal like that of Roger Williams was doubtless accelerated by the hostility of his neighbours, he journeyed some hundred miles eastward and spent his life in pastoral and itinerant preaching among other seacoast villages. Traces of him are not altogether obliterated. He was known as Elder Lord, and he seems to have been as uncompromising as he was tireless. It is not difficult to imagine him breaking the ice of pond or of harbour to immerse anxious converts, who for their souls' safety dared not tarry until a more clement season.

Perhaps the best record of this stern doer of the Word, of his indefatigable energy and robust, unrelenting piety, is read in his son, my great-grandfather, Heard Lord, born in 1806 and destined to become at once the corner-stone and the pillar of the

Baptist Church, organized that very year in Blue
Hill. Whether his quaint name was given him in
hope and in prophecy, no one can say; surely he not
only heard the Lord but hearkened unto Him. My
mother, whom he took into his home upon the early
death of her mother and the subsequent removal of
her father to Massachusetts, has seen to it that his
life and character have not passed into oblivion.

He himself was of no small education. Largely
self-taught and an omnivorous reader, he was known
not only in his own community but elsewhere as a
man of parts. While still in his twenties, he became a
schoolmaster and spent the greater part of his long
life in teaching the village schools along the coast of
eastern Maine. According to the custom of that day,
he "boarded round," a week in one home, a week in
another, food and lodging being given him as a due
part of his salary. To add further to his support and
to that of his family, from whom he was necessarily
absent for long periods, he taught singing-schools in
the evenings, instructing his students "how to render
those noble hymns of Mr. Isaac Watts and upon occasion a few lighter, harmless melodies much to their
taste." He was also, as occasion offered and necessity
demanded, both a carpenter and a shoemaker, always
carrying with him his chest of tools and a supply of
leather. His shrewdness must have dictated in many
cases not only the making but also the keeping of
wooden forms for the feet he shod; for an examina-
tion of his old chest a few years back revealed dozens

of such moulds, each carefully marked with the name and the address of its owner. To the year of his death in 1887 he fashioned his own shoes and those of his immediate family.

The too few letters which have been preserved testify to his interests and anxieties. He is concerned over the uncertainty of his son, my grandfather, "as regards his conversion," but relieved by his apparent industry; he writes of a ten-mile walk mostly at night "to relieve the passing and to strengthen the faith of a former student dying of brain fever"; he is distressed over the rise in prices at the time of the Civil War but far more distressed over the dishonesty of a country shop-keeper, whom he must needs fear "to be a backslider from his profession"; he would gladly have his wife purchase herself a new gown "of the best stuff, not too gaudy." His books, a mere handful, reveal his enthusiasms and his thoughts: Fontenelle's *Plurality of Worlds*, Milton's *Paradise Lost*, Thomson's *Seasons*, Izaak Walton's *Compleat Angler*, William Law's *Serious Call to a Devout and Holy Life*, the tragedies of Shakespeare complete in one tiny and almost unreadable volume, Richard Baxter's *Saints' Everlasting Rest*, *The History of the United States to 1840, with Moral and Religious Reflections Thereon*, Cotton Mather's *Wonders of the Invisible World*, *The Genuine Works of Josephus*, published in 1828, *The Pilgrim's Progress*. On the fly leaf of each he has penned his name in clear, full letters, Heard Lord, and beneath it he has fixed a scroll of intricate design.

Retiring from teaching when he was sixty, he spent the last twenty years of his life with his books, his small farm, and occasional work at building or at making shoes. These years remain fresh and firm in my mother's mind, for it was then that she was under his care as a child and young girl. She pictures him at his desk in his black stock and cravat, his long frock coat, and his self-made shoes, absorbed for hours at a time in some huge commentary on the Scriptures, borrowed from the Baptist parson. Like Hazlitt's father a half century earlier, he was pondering over the age of Methuselah, "a mighty speculation," guessing at the shape of Noah's ark or considering the riches of Solomon's temple. He hated and feared the reading of fiction. Even the great English novelists of his own day he distrusted; and the scorn which he meted out to popular favourites was withering. My mother dared not in his presence avow her guilty love for E. P. Roe or the tears she shed in secret over *Queechy* and *The Wide, Wide World!*

Above all he detested the changes which even in his day he saw creeping steadily over the face of the society he knew. He regarded innovation as a lack of courtesy toward what was old and tried; and he set himself to right such disrespect wherever he could. My mother cites as illustration of this trait the following story of his politeness:

In the seventies a custom long common among churches was abandoned, that of the congregation

turning to face the members of the choir as they sang
the hymns from the rear gallery. The practice was
suddenly seen to connote a lamentable mark of disrespect toward the pulpit and its occupant; and the
churches hastened to rectify their unseemly behaviour. But my great-grandfather quietly refused to
fall into this new line. Perhaps the memory of the
courtesy accorded him as a singing-master constrained him; perhaps his veneration for Mr. Watts's
noble hymns prompted his action. At all events, as
the Doxology was sung, as the morning hymns were
announced, he consistently arose and, turning in his
seat, faced the choir in the gallery, his fine bass voice,
probably swelling with righteous indignation, supplementing and complementing their praises and
petitions. My mother cites, too, her own mortification and that of her grandmother upon such occasions, their mutual dread of Sunday morning. But he
asked or commanded no support from his family. He
himself acted as he thought seemly and right, and he
never forsook his principle until his last illness kept
him from the church. Surely such courage of conviction, even in a lesser matter, should not go unchronicled!

(2)

The women of my mother's family, like practically
all women prior to the late nineteenth century, left
no marks of distinction for the emancipated minds of
their present descendants to treasure. They have
passed in that long, hooded procession, stretching

back through hundreds of years, of those who counted their lives well lost in the salvation of their husbands and sons from complete oblivion, who for themselves cultivated the necessary virtues of meekness, self-abnegation, and patience. The wife of the early and middle nineteenth century in rural communities knew or expected no life of her own. To this common lot the sole exception lay in the case of the woman who, married into a seafaring family, might be taken by her husband on a foreign voyage probably before the advent of many children. To share the captain's cabin, to mend, knit, or embroider on the quarter deck through long, sunny days, to provide virtuous inspiration for the sailors and lesser officers, and above all to be freed from the thousand nagging cares of a household—what must these things have meant to certain fortunate female souls? But such instances, none too common at best, cannot be termed typical; and my mother's family, unlike that of my father, was not a seafaring one.

My mother's mother died in her early thirties, a prey to consumption, which in the last century took its ghastly toll throughout all seacoast communities; her maternal grandmother likewise. Of the grandmother in whose care she was reared, the wife of the redoubtable Heard, she recalls little that was singular or unusual. Her name was Serena, and she seems never to have forsaken its connotation. "My grandmother," writes my mother, "constantly effaced herself in her care for my grandfather. Her first thought

was for him and his comfort; and I never knew her
to speak or to act contrary to his wishes. She was a
woman of a lovely nature, a perfect housekeeper, and
she saw to it that nothing about the care or supervision of the home should ever irritate her husband.
She adored him to the day of his death, two years
before her own, and after it wanted nothing except
to join him." A description which might well fit ten
thousand times ten thousand of her contemporaries!

My mother herself belonged to a happier generation. Born in 1866, she heard even in her isolated
community of the growing popularity and prestige of
the Female Seminaries, of the founding of colleges
for women. She witnessed the wider entrance of her
sex into the teaching profession; and she gathered, in
spite of the dubious prophesyings of her elders, that
the door of life was not completely shut in the face
of the girl who did not choose or was, unhappily, not
chosen to marry.

She learned, too, upon her entrance at the age of
twelve into the Blue Hill Academy, that young
women might excel young men in their studies. Becoming early proficient in Latin, she continued in her
study of it, her grandfather being convinced that such
study was well worth the weekly tuition of thirty-
five cents as over against that of twenty cents paid by
non-classical scholars. Upon her graduation at the
age of sixteen she taught two terms of district school,
receiving gratefully and without question five dollars
weekly for the first and five dollars and fifty cents

for the second. Thereafter she was invited back to the Academy to assist in the instruction of Latin Grammar and Cicero; and she went with pride and dignity to teach young men who dreamed of Bowdoin College while they sawed and split a winter wood-pile. While she taught, she studied, storing away the orations against Catiline and the six books of the *Æneid* in a mind so retentive that to this day she can assist her grandchildren.

At just eighteen she married my father, five years her senior. Her first child came close upon her nineteenth birthday, her eighth not far from her forty-sixth. Of her life spent in the nurture and upbringing of her five daughters and three sons, of her vitality and her humour, of her eager co-operation in her husband's profession, of her interest and participation in the thought and the reading of three generations, the following chapters will bear inadequate witness.

CHAPTER III

MY FATHER'S FAMILY

(1)

MY father, as I have said, came of seafaring stock. Early in the history of Blue Hill his grandfather and his great-uncles sailed the seas, those of lesser ambitions clinging to the coast trade in their smaller vessels, those of greater becoming early the masters of full-rigged ships which cut the waters of every ocean. Such an inheritance, although in no sense rare among New Englanders, is rightly cherished. For, in Sarah Orne Jewett's fine phrase, such men did not mistake their native parishes for the whole of the world instead of a part thereof. Their sense of values was neither subjective nor circumscribed. While they sailed, they gave to their children and grandchildren the example as well as the knowledge of endurance and of courage, of resiliency after disaster, of the satisfaction of playing a game with Fortune, provided one were well fortified by nature and by training for such a gamble. When they left the sea to enjoy their waning years in peace and relative prosperity, they brought to their homes and to their communities a perspective and a power of evaluation which has left its mark on succeeding

27

generations. The maritime life of America, particularly of New England which knew it best, gave its chief contribution to the country in the character of the men whom it made. Its methods were ruthless, but its prophecies were sure. In these latter days one looks vainly for a worthy substitute.

My grandfather, Captain Melatiah Kimball Chase, in common with others of his family began his seafaring young. By the age of twenty-four he had first officer's papers and an honourable past. In the year 1847 he shipped as mate on a brig carrying corn to the starving Irish. Of that ill-fated voyage, of the loss of the brig and all on board except himself— a loss which included his brother as second mate— account will be given in chapters especially devoted to life at sea. Undaunted by such misfortune, he continued to sail, becoming two years later the master of his own ship.

My grandmother, Eliza Ann Wescott, was the one woman of my family whose life in those years uneventful for her sex was not destined to be bounded by the trivial affairs of an isolated Maine village. From the very beginning her fortune seemed governed by peculiarly exciting stars. She was one of those thrice blessed individuals who seem born to have things happen to them, who attract experiences as a magnet attracts steel. Moreover, in her own mind at least she was fortified at the start by a more distinguished ancestry than had been allotted to others of my progenitors. Wescotts had fought with

William the Conqueror and thereby received titles and lands. They had some centuries later married with the Lyttletons and therefrom had added to their prestige. Her mother, too, in my grandmother's eager imagination had contributed not a little by being a Lowell of Cambridge; and although rumour had it that her branch of the family had not been held in the high regard attributed to those remaining in Massachusetts, she herself was never known to admit that probability!

Rich as her middle and later life was to be in memory and in wide associations, the surroundings of her childhood were simple enough. Surely no distinction of ancestry was apparent about the barren upland farm where, the eldest of ten children, she was reared. Even the relative comforts and conveniences of village life one hundred years ago were denied her. She knew what it was, not merely to work but to labour unremittingly in the care and upbringing of a large family, in the toil of an unproductive farm five miles from anywhere at all. She knew only the bare necessities of body and of mind. Two dresses yearly, self-fashioned after she was eight, one of calico at three cents the yard for summer, one of stuff for winter, spun and woven by her own fingers. One pair of shoes, for winter only, made by the village cobbler and destined for long endurance regardless of the growth of feet.

Yet even in her earliest years she seems to have possessed a prodigality of nature, a wealth of energy and initiative that transcended hardships into pleasurable tests of her capacities and endowments. "I was happy as a child," she used to say when, distressed by the easy lot of her grandchildren in the nineties, she was impelled to count her early blessings. "Time never hung heavy on *my* hands. *I* never had to ask my mother what I might do. I loved hard work, for I could show how smart I was!"

"Smart," indeed, she must have been. When we thought ourselves encumbered by many chores (for ours, like all other country families thirty years ago, was a co-operative one) she recounted her labours of a certain Saturday which marked her tenth birthday. Her father and mother having driven early to the village for necessary supplies and some rare visits with friends, she did the usual household tasks, superintending meanwhile six children younger than herself. By eleven in the morning she had in addition churned and made up ten pounds of butter; by noon she had fed the family and two farm-hands besides. The dinner dishes washed, she was seized with a desire to surprise her parents upon their return. Whereupon from an old coat of her father's she cut and fashioned a new suit, coat, waistcoat, and trousers complete, for her brother John aged five, and at four o'clock had him proudly dressed therein and stationed on exhibition in the best room! The orange, which was brought her as a birthday gift and which was the first she had ever seen, she must have eaten with triumph before crawling under her self-made patchwork quilt that night!

On Sundays she walked with her brothers and sisters the five miles to and from the Congregational Church. Between April and November she carried in her hand her shoes and the white stockings she herself had knit, and upon sight of the church washed her feet in a wayside brook and donned them, for the service only, walking back in the selfsame manner she had come.

She learned early to make all sorts of beverages and cordials, dandelion, elderberry, and blackberry wines, raspberry shrub, heartening winter drinks from sarsaparilla and checkerberry. In the spring, up to her last years, she concocted a beer from spruce and fir tips, mysteriously stirring these ingredients plus every manner of herb and evergreen berry into boiling water and yeast and allowing all to stand in a great earthen crock for three days in a cool buttery. The primeval tang and fragrance of this mixture, for which she would never give the recipe, made her justly renowned among her acquaintances.

At fifteen she left her upland farm to become a midwife both in the village and through outlying districts. Doubtless she had learned her profession well, if prematurely, through her necessary assistance at the advent of her own brothers and sisters. At seventeen, sitting on her diminutive horsehair trunk in the back of an accommodating farm wagon, she journeyed the thirty miles to Bangor to learn the trade of a seamstress, thereafter returning to sew at twenty-five cents a day in families which were better off than her own even though they could perhaps boast of no such predecessors.

At twenty-two in April of the year 1847 the world opened wide for her eager embrace. Singing in the church choir one afternoon "in a pink calico dress and a straw poke bonnet with pink roses beneath the brim," she met the admiring gaze of a young sailor but lately wrecked off Ireland and the sole survivor of a disastrous voyage. The service was in a peculiar sense his own, for as was common among seacoast communities it was held to commemorate those who had perished from that ill-starred passage. "A Mighty Fortress Is Our God" was the hymn; and the surrender of the young sailor was complete!

While he continued at sea, rising steadily toward his goal as master, she continued to fashion wide-skirted dresses of percale and muslin, bombazine and taffeta, forsaking this livelihood only as families, which had known her earlier ministrations, obeyed the ancient command to increase and multiply. The journal which he kept for her, sending it back by infrequent mail-packets or by returning ships as rare occasion offered, bears witness to his life and thoughts, as also to himself as a young man who had dreamed over his speller:

"We are now nearing Gibraltor which point we trust to make on the morrow. Although we have been much thretened with mutiny from our Chinees crew, the dangar has subsided. The voyage has been verry uneasy and hard. I think allways of you in my night watches. I am greatful in that you are willing to share my life which I have choosen before others which might be happier for you."

In 1849 they were married and thereupon journeyed to New York to board his ship. Of her life at sea, the disaster of her wedding journey, the widening prospects afforded her by tarrying in foreign ports, Marseilles, Cadiz, Shanghai, of her walks with her little girls along a ship's deck instead of along Maine roads, following pages will chronicle. Still young when the outbreak of the war in 1861 advised a return to life at home, she took up her less stimulating if more secure ways as a housekeeper and a mother.

Here as on shipboard were made manifest that tireless energy, that resiliency from ill fortune, that extraordinary youthfulness, which quickened all her days until she died at eighty-seven and which brightened even the stillness of her face in death. The great white house with broad roofs and hospitable fireplaces received hundreds of guests through its picket gate. Her stories of sharks and storms, sea-serpents and flying-fish, Spanish cavaliers and Chinese temples grew with each recital in richness of detail. One suspected her of being unable to tell the exact truth, much as she extolled it, her regard for it being at all times æsthetic and dramatic rather than intrinsic. But with all her delight in the experiences with which she had been favoured, she retained a breadth of vision which kept her horizons wide and clear. Her eyes, though they shone with excitement over the Sargasso Sea, shone also with larger desire for the future of her children.

Her two eldest, the little girls whom she had taken on her voyages, died young. Her remaining daughter she sent to Mount Holyoke Seminary, proud of her early love of "deep" books, a love which she herself had never kept still long enough to nurture. Her one son, my father, was her earthly idol, and she saw to it that no advantage of mind or of spirit should be closed to him.

The God she believed in was perforce an exciting Deity, who performed stupendous miracles at sea and less appealing ones on shore. Puritanism was surely not native to her temperament; but it had been too well ingrafted in her early years for her ever entirely to escape its clutches. She talked much about "that straight and narrow path that leadeth unto life" and outwardly travelled it in the most seemly fashion. Inwardly she scaled easier and more delectable mountains. For an hour every Sunday morning she "meditated" in secret, allowing no interruption to avert or to disturb her devotions. Yet the conviction of those who knew her best, that her thoughts were quite as often in Cadiz as in Heaven, was not to be gainsaid. Certain it is that, her meditation over, she turned with avidity to the details of dressing for church, which she entered at ten-thirty, always in a spectacular and surely not an unconscious manner.

She read her Bible diligently, knowing it by heart from Genesis to Revelation. Her chief delight therein was the Acts of the Apostles, as indeed her consuming delight was in anything active. The unhappy and dramatic fate of Ananias and Sapphira; the awful pronouncement against Elymas, the Sorcerer; the raising from death of Tabitha, that nimble maker of coats and garments; the hair-raising conversion of Saint Paul on the Damascus road—such incidents as these were constantly on her lips as words of exhortation against idleness and warnings against sin. The lamentations or the kindling assurances of Job and of the major prophets were never *her* meat and drink. She read elsewhere also with ardour and absorption, inclining toward romances and effectually silencing her conscience against any possible harm therein. Her taste was not literary; she liked a book to move quickly, to encourage laughter and tears. E. P. Roe gave place in her declining years to Mary J. Holmes and Bertha M. Clay; F. Marion Crawford and Frank Stockton were her bedside companions; no tale of Anna Catherine Green or of A. Conan Doyle escaped her. And if perchance she ever felt an uneasy stirring within her breast, she could always turn again to the pious, yet lively, acts of her beloved Apostles or upon sombre occasions to the melancholy ethics of Henry Wadsworth Longfellow in *The Psalm of Life*.

(2)

The only son of fond parents, who by the date of his birth in 1861 had acquired sufficient means to make his early path secure, my father was born with the proverbial silver spoon in his mouth. Times had summarily changed since his father's day; and with the growing use of steam the sea afforded fewer chances for pre-eminence. At eleven he was sent to school in a neighbouring town where a Grammar School, conducted rather after the English fashion, had been established. Early proficient and eager in his studies, he went at fourteen to the Classical Institute at Hallowell on the Kennebec to prepare for Bowdoin College, it being held that such preparation away from home redounded somewhat to a family's prestige and position.

According to his own self-analysis in later years and to the testimony of two of his Hallowell teachers, who are still living,[1] he was by no means wholly a student. Indeed, more than one hurried trip of his parents to the school to extricate him from non-academic difficulties add proof to assertion. He was apparently bright but none too diligent, although he was at all times an insatiate reader. He hated mathematics and the elementary sciences then taught and spent the time allotted to his studies with the classics and with English literature and composition. Not having completed his necessary reading of Greek by

[1] The Reverend Frederick A. Wilson of Andover, Massachusetts, and Professor A. J. Burr of Beloit, Wisconsin.

the June preceding his entrance to college in 1882, he spent that summer in the town of Waldoboro reading Homer with the Congregational minister of that place. His *Iliad* and his *Odyssey* with their marginal dates bear witnesses to his daily progresses with Achilles and Odysseus.

But although he did not conclude his college course, my father's love for books and study became the consuming passion of his life. At home he was literally never without a book. Taking up the law as a profession after his early marriage and reading with the firm of Wiswell and King in the neighbouring city of Ellsworth, he read, not law but everything else on his weekly drives of fourteen miles to and from Blue Hill. He read at his solitary breakfasts which he always ate apart from his family and later than they; for, since he read half the night, he rose not before eight. He read in his office when he should have been at Blackstone; he read during the long evenings while we studied our lessons. He believed and practised his faith that books and the resources therefrom are not only the sole proof against the slings and arrows of fortune but the one sure solace of life.

History was his major interest. As his mother adored the incidents, the drama, of fiction, so he adored the facts of history, seeing in the most prosaic of them the older, finer meaning of *fact*, an *act* or a *deed*. He had an extraordinary, almost miraculous memory for dates. I remember his disappointment and chagrin when, upon a vacation return from college, I gave in response to his question the date of Napoleon's birth as 1759 instead of 1769. He liked nothing so much as to question his children as to the times of great events, skipping agilely and without comment from the third Ptolemy to the Kansas-Nebraska Bill. He required that we memorize early the names and dates both of the Kings of England and the Presidents of the United States and that we frequently recite each list together with the counties of Maine, the alphabetized countries of Asia, the twelve Apostles according to Saint Matthew, and the rulers of the Kingdoms of Israel. He transmuted mere information into something enthralling, something to harbour and to cherish as food for thought and reflection. From him I gained a reverence for the retentive powers of the human mind for which I can never be sufficiently grateful.

And yet I must guard against the impression that my father's knowledge and interest were merely, even largely encyclopedic. As I have said, he prized facts not for themselves but for the opportunity they afforded for thought and reflection. It is true that he held the exercise of the memory to be intellectual wealth and trained his children unceasingly therein; it is more true that he saw nothing as isolated, that he possessed the Coleridgean type of imagination which in its synthetic and magical power brings all things into relationship one with another. Thus we were early trained also to compare, to relate, to distinguish the effects of causes and the causes of effects.

"If you," asked my father, "had suffered as Napoleon did at the military school in Brienne, what feelings would have been uppermost in your mind when you became a corporal in the French army?" or,

"If Ulysses S. Grant and Robert E. Lee had sat down to dinner as enemies, what subjects might they have found to talk about which would have made them friendly toward each other?" or again,

"What, do you suppose, would have interested Queen Elizabeth the most could she have lived long enough to come to Virginia in 1607?"

Next to history, my father's love was strongest for the classics, especially for Greek. He knew innumerable lines of the *Iliad* and the *Odyssey*, which he recited as he dressed in the morning and thundered out, provided he were in a talkative mood, as he descended the stairs for breakfast. Thus we caught early the sound and the fascination alike of Greek hexameters and looked forward to the day when we also might recite them.

He was a quiet man and in many respects a stern one. My mother used to guard him against our annoyance and us against his displeasure. He insisted upon what would be called today a rather stilted perfection of manner. We always addressed him as *Sir*, punctuating any continued conversation with him with a liberal sprinkling of the term. He could not tolerate a whining voice and preferred a scream of rage to sniffling or to sulkiness. Like Lucian, whom he read and admired, he sensed the dignity of extremes.

In religion he was in no sense orthodox; I suppose his theology was Unitarian. But he held tenaciously to the necessity of a thorough knowledge of the Bible, not in the Puritan sense of the indispensable familiarity with the unalterable and all-sufficient Word of God but rather as the mark of an educated person and as a safe guide to dignified and decent conduct. He took a humorous delight in outdistancing the village ministers in his Scriptural knowledge and accuracy. Up to his last years—he died at the early age of fifty-one—he attended the Congregational Church, timing the morning sermon and not infrequently remonstrating with the preacher on Monday when the discourse was over long.

He cared nothing for society and rarely spent an evening away from his library. Perhaps he held with Parson Adams that, knowing books, he knew mankind as well; perhaps he felt with Bacon that men of higher stature lived therein "without delusion or imposture." Aside from his reading, his wife and his children, he loved animals, horses, dogs, the family cow and cat. I remember once seeing his eyes fill with tears as during an illness my mother read him from some history the description of the wounded and dying horses at the battle of Waterloo.

His chief interest, so far as his children were con-

cerned, lay in the storage and the discipline of their
minds; and he tested and admonished, I feel certain,
not so much because of his pride in their excellency
in their studies as because of his passionate desire that
they should discover the ecstatic pleasure which was
his. Surely he lived in the "enfranchised world" of
old Richard de Bury, the "substantial world" of
Wordsworth. I shall always see him, a big dark man,
sunk in his great chair, one unquiet hand upon his
forehead, the other quietly turning the pages of
Creasy's *Fifteen Decisive Battles of the World*, or
Froissart's *Chronicles of England, France, and Spain*,
or Macaulay's *History*, or his own old *Iliad* and
Odyssey with his annotations at eighteen—those
marginal dates of his progress "in the realms of
gold" in those days when he was glimpsing the wide
and far reaches of that "pleasaunt land" which was
to be his life.

CHAPTER IV

CHORES AND THEIR BY-PRODUCTS

TO lovers of the long and intricate history of language the disuse and final death of certain words is a matter of regret. Yet every age bears witness to the inevitableness of such loss. One cannot, for instance, without a smile speak of gasoline as *fodder* or refer to the replenishment of one's kitchenette during National Canned Goods Week as the buying of *provender*. Since modesty is no longer a "candle to merit," as it was in the mind of Fielding, what need have we for such adjectives as *comely* and *demure*? And how can one with any sense either of perspective or of humour who lies under his automobile and dickers with its works refer to his occupation as a *chore*?

Specialists in dialect tell us that *chore* is largely an American word. In England, where it is limited to an unenviable class of society, it is usually spelt and pronounced with an *a*. They tell us, too (one trusts sadly), that here it has become colloquial, relegated to rural communities which find it a necessary adjunct to common speech. Gone are the days when Emerson suggested the doing of *chores* as an assistance to the seclusion and the reflection of the would-be scholar!

But thirty years ago the word was in reputable, indeed, indispensable use among all families of average means, both rural and urban. Just as reputable and indispensable were the chores themselves, those little, odd, miscellaneous pieces of business which must be performed if the wheels of family life were to turn freely. Indeed, so important were they to the integrity of life and living that an early chapter becomes their right. In ours, as in all other families which we knew, chores were part of the accepted routine of the day. Like the talents of the parable they were allotted to each of us according to his several abilities, and remonstrances were not anticipated.

"May we coast in Dr. Grindle's field this morning?" we were wont to ask at a January breakfast.

"It will be time to settle that matter," said my mother, "when your chores are finished."

Now the essence of chores lay in their co-operative character. In this they were sharply distinguished from jobs of all kinds. One was paid for a job but never for a chore. The performance of the former connoted agreement and consent; the performance of the latter, participation and partnership. For example, my driving of Constancy, the family cow, to and from her distant pasture twice a day, from April to November, in all weathers was a job. I was paid five dollars for it on the first of every November between the ages of ten and fifteen. The money was mine to use as I liked, and, although I was generally impelled by the attitude and example of my parents to

put it in the savings bank, I was never actually constrained to do so. On the contrary, my feeding of the
pig was a chore. Its fulfilment required no unreasonable amount of time or effort and was regarded simply as a portion of my share in the comfort and ex-
pediency of family life. Likewise, my other morning
and evening tasks about the barn, for which I ever
had a greater predilection than for tasks about the
house, were chores—the feeding of the horses, the
bedding of the cow, the weekly sweeping of the floor
when I became large and strong enough to wield the
broom. The carrying of a morning quart of milk to
a neighbour, the daily fetching of a dozen eggs (at
ten cents a dozen!) from Mrs. Douglass on the hill,
the filling of the wood-boxes in kitchen, library, and
bed-rooms, the piling of wood and the splitting of it,
when axes became safe instruments, the shovelling of
snow, the fall gathering of apples—these, too, were
chores, to be performed by one or another of us
cheerfully and without question. Often the assignment of these was varied month by month; sometimes we enjoyed the dramatic device of drawing for
them on slips of paper shaken in a hat. But the idea
that they were more than our just and due service
never once occurred to us. Nor could we be stirred
to any possible rebellion by our associates, for every
child we knew contributed in precisely the same manner to the well-being of his own household.

Indoors, a large and growing family with at most
one "hired girl" necessitated other and less interest-

ing chores. Lamps must be filled and cleaned, the black wicks, disagreeable alike to nose and fingers, cut in a circular fashion to insure a steady light, and the polished chimneys covered with brown paper bags and arranged in an orderly row upon the shelf above the kitchen sink. Dishes, an interminable number, must be dried with no dampness and with no breakage; beds must be made. Dust clothes must follow the intricacies of Victorian table legs and the small, triangular shelves of what-nots.

Ruleless babies multiplied chores in an almost incredible fashion, even before they began to be peripatetic and hence to demand active and ceaseless guardianship from some older sister or brother. Up to a year old, in those days before Dr. Emmett Holt revolutionized their nurture, their daily naps were a matter of deepest concern and anxiety, for upon such naps depended the even life of the family. It is safe to say that ninety per cent of the infant population of the nineties was swung or rocked in cradles. One, indeed, is given to wondering if the aversion felt by many middle-aged persons to syncopated music might not have been unconsciously engendered by those longer, smoother rhythms to which they were daily accustomed in their infancy!

To one chore made necessary by the presence of five brothers and sisters younger than I at the age of fifteen, I shall always be grateful. On Saturday mornings and on week days during the long winter vacations, which because of municipal poverty were given us from February to April, I was stationed at nine o'clock in the library before the baby's cradle. My task was simple. By judicious swayings of the cradle I was to keep the baby asleep surely for two and, if possible, for three hours, while in the kitchen beyond things continued on their wonted and orderly way. I was never averse to this chore; in fact, it became so coveted that in order to secure its allotment I was willing to resort to bribery. For in those long, slow hours I could read, exempt from any charge of idleness which sometimes fell upon those who devoured books during working time.

I prepared for the graduate school by that cradle. Today when college freshmen confess to an ignorance of the Waverley novels or *Scottish Chiefs*, *Lorna Doone* or *Great Expectations*, I am lenient, remembering that their brothers and sisters were never rocked. My parents were wise enough to prohibit few books, only seeing to it that nothing on our family shelves was inadvisable or harmful. When I had exhausted our none too abundant store, I borrowed from every house in town, from the Ladies' Social Library, and from the few rather pious volumes lent every week by the Superintendent of the Sunday School. I read Shakespeare, Thackeray, George Eliot; William Black, Dickens, and the Brontës; Hawthorne, Cooper, and Robert Louis Stevenson. I do not remember that I was conscious of any difference in treatment between *Bleak House* and *Little Women*, between George Eliot and

Sophie May, that I regarded one as duller than the other, more difficult to "get into." They were all stories. If they took me into a different world and kind from the one I knew, I gloried in the swift and certain transference; if they related experiences I had had, I felt a pleasurable sense of companionship and sympathy.

One set of books, now doubtless passed out of circulation, I recall with especial pleasure, the biographies and historical sketches of J. S. C. Abbott. These, much to my regret, we did not own; but I borrowed them volume by volume, covered each with the brown paper we were required to wrap about all borrowed books, read and reread before a reluctant return. Probably these were inaccurate and sentimental; it is difficult, indeed, to credit such a prolific writer as Mr. Abbott with both accuracy and objectiveness; but they opened doors to me into new periods and civilizations—Greece and Rome, the Renaissance, Spain, the French Revolution—and I shall never forget them.

Mr. Abbott, too, possessed an added value in that the perusal of his books pleased my father. When he tiptoed in at noon, if perchance the baby had been induced to sleep so late, and looked over my shoulder as he invariably did, I was sure to receive a more reassuring nod than that provoked by *Five Little Peppers*. I was, in point of fact, more than once guilty of a swift substitution at the eleventh hour. Seeing him walking up the driveway and being desirous for one reason or another of his heartiest approval, I often hastily hid *Jo's Boys* beneath the chair cushion and became engrossed in Creasy or Froissart or John Fiske, gentlemen without the charm, exuberance, and vivacity of Mr. Abbott or of Charles Dickens in *A Child's History of England*.

Much, of course, of the morning's absorption depended upon the baby; and many were the savage impulses I restrained when he or she woke at the wrong moment and demanded attention. Thus the sight of *The Lay of the Last Minstrel* will ever be attended by a feeling of exasperation, for the child in question refused to sleep longer precisely at the moment for the opening of the grave of Michael Scott in Melrose Abbey and the rash seizure of the Mighty Book by William of Deloraine! I remember only once in those years of reading when I woke the baby myself, desperate in the great silent room for company. That was upon the occasion of my completion of *Wuthering Heights*, which Stevenson calls "that powerful, miserable novel." And, indeed, I confess to that same desire for company more than once in later readings of that miraculous book, written—how could she have done it?—by a half-crazed girl of twenty-four.

Another chore made necessary by the ever-present baby was the nightly putting him to bed at six o'clock. This was in no sense so delightful as sitting by his cradle, and I recall it only because of its recurrence over a period of many years. Perhaps, too, the participation therein of every member of the family, except my father, caused it to partake generously of the inherent nature of a chore.

The procession started in the kitchen, the baby having been undressed, dried and swathed in night clothes and blankets by the kitchen stove. My mother bore her youngest. She was preceded by my oldest sister who, as attendant acolyte, and by reason of her age entrusted before the others of us, carried a lamp, lighted in winter, in summer ready for lighting. I followed my mother with a large pan, which contained the baby's bottles, his milk, and a small tin cup for heating the same over the lamp in question. My sister, two years my junior, grasped in one hand a creosote burner and in the other a tiny bottle of creosote against the croup, which might make its insidious appearance without the slightest warning. My brother brought up the rear of the line with an armful of extra blankets and diapers. We stopped for a moment in the library for my father to look with pride and approbation upon the baby and then went our way up the long, curving stairs. We did not think it strange that my father took no part in the evening rite. Early we took it for granted that he, like the other fathers we knew, was supposed to be manually ineffective so far as life indoors was concerned.

As the years went on, the procession changed character, my brother being released as soon as a younger sister was old enough to take his place. In those days the work of women and the work of men were in more distinct categories than they are today. Only I continued with my chores in the stable, my mother consenting on the ground that I was of less service in the house. But without or within we did our share toward the common weal.

Chores over-reached themselves in their by-products. In our family as in all others each child was made to feel himself necessary to a larger group. If he went away for an infrequent visit, he saw to it that the performance of his chores was well arranged for before his departure. Although his individuality was not stressed as it is today, although in the average family he was seldom regarded as singular or problematical, his co-operative value was tacitly admitted and encouraged. His assistance was taken for granted, and his willingness as well. In some rare cases it may have happened that children were over-worked, that they were made to feel a responsibility incompatible with their years. But at all events selfishness did not flourish under such a system. As for me, recalling Mr. J. S. C. Abbott and my father's approving nod over my eagerness for Froissart and realizing that in those years between eight and seventeen I did fifty per cent of all the reading of my life, I can only return thanks for the chores that were required of me and for their inestimable by-products.

CHAPTER V

ANIMALS AS FAMILY RETAINERS

MY father was, as I have said, a great lover of animals. He was forever bringing home at all hours of the day or night some unfortunate beast which needed temporary attention or permanent residence. He excused his indulgence therein to my mother on the ground that the care and companionship of such creatures were good for us children; but as a matter of fact I am sure his own inclination and satisfaction were the more powerful factors. My mother, harassed as she doubtless was over these importations, made few remonstrances, quietly consenting in the winter to boxes and baskets of various sorts around the kitchen stove and near the registers and fireplaces of the living-rooms. I remember once that she did object mildly when she was aroused in the night to attend the wants of a cosset lamb which my father had found bleating on some country road as he returned late one evening from holding court. And I recall, too, her confusion when our tame crow Jim picked out her hair-pins while she was spreading the Monday washing on the grass of the field. But for the most part she, like us, regarded these inmates of the house or the stable, whether transient or permanent, merely to be taken for granted.

51

For that matter our family was in no sense unique in its possession of pets, even though no other father whom we knew shared the collector's avarice of our own. The doctor's family next door had innumerable guinea-pigs and a goat which was constantly butting some child into the ditch; the *Blue Hill House* on the corner was overrun with cats of every hue and disposition; one of our friends had a tame wood-chuck under the barn, a collie which daily threatened its miserable life, pigeons galore, and a dozen white rats.

My mother drew the line at white rats. She held them to be the purveyors of disease and dirt, and her good housekeeping revolted at the very mention of them. But they were the only creatures she set her face against. At one time she suffered uncomplain-ingly two dogs (a setter named Captain and a terrier, Ezekiel), a cat, Dolly Moses, with at least two fam-ilies a year, a lamb, Lucy, a baby pig with a broken back but a great hold on life, who was nurtured for weeks in her one clothes-basket, and a pair of rabbits named Admiral Dewey and Clara Barton. These last grievously disappointed us and denied their traditi-tional abilities by having no offspring. Perhaps, in-deed, a Special Providence answered my mother's prayers, for doubtless they are the one such pair on record.

Such creatures as these had the run of the house whenever they wished and, being continually in her way, came more or less directly under my mother's supervision, although the care of them was included in our chores. In the barn the more substantial of our retainers were housed. Like practically all the other householders in the village, my father kept horses, at all times one, usually two. In these he took great pride especially on Sunday afternoons, for, weather permitting, we went on a family drive behind them.

This drive partook of the nature of a function rather than of a pastime. In the first place, my father was insistent that every member of the family, unless in disgrace because of some misbehaviour, should accompany him; in the second place, we wore our Sunday clothes and our most dignified manners; in the third place, we were bound to meet other equipages, for the Sunday drive was a custom among all those possessing the means thereof, and we could tacitly compare our consolidated appearance with theirs. My father sat up very straight in the driver's seat, the reins in his left hand, in his right the whip which he held high across the reins, making it inscribe an acute angle in relation to them. With his whip hand he raised his hat gravely to the occupants of the carriages past which we rolled or jingled, according to the season. At such moments I am sure he was guilty of the sin of pride in all its manifold ramifications—pride in his family, in his superior turnout, even in himself as a fine figure of a man. Perhaps DeQuincey, going down with victory on the English mail-coach, knew no greater exhilaration! As for us, our

family sense as we swept by our neighbours was overwhelming.

In the summer our vehicle was a surrey or a carry-
all, in the winter a two-seated pung, painted bright
yellow and well-equipped on the shafts with bells to
add to the jingling belts which the horses wore. My
mother held the youngest of us; two of the half
sizes sat on small stools between the back and the
front seat; the older among us occupied with gravity
and decorum the places beside our parents.

The horses were always specially groomed for this
occasion, not infrequently by my father himself.
They stepped high and held their heads erect, they,
too, seemingly influenced by the unique character of
the situation. When we talked at all (for we were
too much impressed by ourselves, by the family solidarity we represented, to chat easily) we commented
upon one or the other of them, upon Lady's unfortunate spavin or Ginger's capricious unwillingness to
pull her half of the load. All in all, both they and
we tacitly agreed that the Sunday drive was an event
not lightly to be entered upon.

Next Ginger's stall in the stable stood Constancy,
the cow, a Jersey of gentle nature and sensitive temperament. She was my chief concern for years, and I
owe her many things. She was a fastidious creature.
I learned to respect her scruples. She liked to stand
for long, contemplative moments between drinks at
the spring half way to her pasture. She never nipped
at alder twigs as she passed them but preferred rather

to browse slowly over a tuft of clover. She always smelled of her grain to be sure she was not being fooled thereby, and she loved the warm bran mash which my father and I prepared for her on bitter evenings. She was never guilty of unseemly hurry. While she loitered on her way to and from home, I loitered with her and learned no small amount concerning spring birds and rare ferns, a knowledge impossible in the company of a more mongrel beast. She was friendly, too, with all her reserve. More than once, injured over some family neglect, real or fancied, I found in her a helpful confidante.

Indeed, in the face of ministrations such as hers it is painful to recall an injury which I once tendered her and from which she suffered intensely. When I was twelve, I proudly conspired with an ingenious youth of the neighbourhood, two years my senior, in the training of a sniffling small boy who was generally and generously despised for his tell-tale and spying tendencies. My superior, looking for an original mode of discipline, procured a supply of snuff, which we administered to our culprit in large doses, taking him for the purpose to Constancy's distant pasture. Becoming thoroughly alarmed by his violent and constant sneezing and fearing that in spite of our threats he would inform our respective parents, we hurried him to the pasture brook to try the curative expedient of holding his nose under water. Unfortunately in our haste we dropped the package of snuff near the fence in a corner favoured by Constancy.

The worst happened. She, hearing my familiar voice in her retreat, drew near in our absence and sniffed eagerly at the overturned contents, apparently filling the sensitive passages of her nose and throat.

Neither I nor my conspirator will ever forget the terror in which we listened to Constancy's first sneezes. There was something antediluvian about those frightful, strangling sounds, shattering the still, hot air of the pasture. Nor shall I ever forget the miserable afternoon and evening which followed; for although the paroxysms diminished with time, she sneezed at intervals during her walk homeward and during her milking. In fact, I woke in the middle of that awful night in a troubled dream of an earthquake to hear again that terrific uproar in the stable and my father's anxious, puzzled comments to my mother in the next room.

The mental agony of that night was hideous; and I confess to the double sins of cowardice and pride. Full of pity as I was for Constancy, full of remorse over my act as author of her dumb pain, I still could be grateful for that dumbness which meant my freedom from the discovery and retribution of a double crime. The warnings of early adolescence already stirring within me would not allow me to confess and thereupon in the eyes of my accomplice become not only unworthy of his confidence and partnership but still young enough for punishment. In a few hours Constancy completely recovered and seemingly in her bountiful nature found no room for ill-will. But

I have always scorned myself for my cowardice toward her who was for so many years my friend.

Not infrequently the ample space in our barn sheltered other residents, sometimes transitory, sometimes not. My father was occasionally a prey to the exigences of his profession. In the family budgets of the eighties and the nineties allowance was not often made for lawyers' fees, and when these had to be met, the debtor often went to his cellar or his stable for the wherewithal. From this sort of barter we, like the doctor's family next door, were the recipients of odd articles and provender. For example, on the day when the doctor received a battered sewing-machine in return for a new baby, we received three kegs of salt mackerel from a fisherman in return for an averted law-suit. Potatoes figured largely in all such deals; and other items of payment which I distinctly remember were clams, lobsters, fowls both dead and alive, books, odd pieces of furniture, turnips, and homemade cheese. Twice cows were brought by farmers to whom my father had rendered some major service; but Constancy received these newcomers with such ill grace that one was summarily sold, the other converted into beef.

Unsatisfactory as was this means and method of business, we children had occasion to bless it in the spring of 1898. The Misses Sarah and Evelina Mansfield, maiden ladies residing in the neighbouring town of Bucksport, owed my father a considerable sum for successfully representing over a term of years their rights in the matter of a boundary line. The case finally tried and won to their greatest satisfaction, they cast about (for they had the highest sense of honour) for sufficient property to cancel their debt, since the payment of fifty dollars in cash was out of the question. The previous year they had received from a renegade brother living in the Far West a small ass, sent, one must believe, as a practical joke and already proving himself an embarrassing possession in more ways than one. Having made overtures to my father, who fell in love with the little beast at first sight, the Misses Mansfield discharged their obligation with dignity and with relief, and we became the possessors of yet another retainer.

It would require pages to chronicle all the countless blessings which we received from Richard Mansfield. He became the retainer of retainers. I was thirteen when he made his advent, and for four years, until I went to college, he was my constant joy. I curried his tough grey hide, cruelly branded on one hind quarter with the letters T.L., letters over which we children held endless cogitations; I drove him twice a year to the blacksmith to have his feet pared (for we never vouchsafed him the expensive dignity of shoes) and each spring to a farmer who clipped his tough winter coat until he was again sleek and slender of outline; I journeyed in his phaëton over miles of country road. He had a habit, deplorable to the precision of the Misses Mansfield but delightful to us, of resting, sometimes for hours, by the wayside. Extremely clever in this operation, he would lie down without the least damage to his shafts or harness, emitting a long and grateful sigh as he stretched out his long neck in the roadside grass and closed his tired eyes. On such occasions my sisters and I read from some pleasant book or did our lessons, sitting beneath a huge green umbrella which was attached in readiness to the back of the seat.

In patience and long-suffering Richard Mansfield was the re-incarnation of the ass who bore the Holy Family into Egypt; and he shared, too, not a little of the responsibility of that thrice happy beast of burden. For, except during his periods of rest, he never shirked his duty or displayed any lack of co-operation. At Thanksgiving, in common with the other animals of the family, he was given an especial feast, his bin on that day being heaped with potatoes, turnips, apples, and carrots (the last always his favourite) and his dessert proffered in the shape of thick, circular slabs of squash and pumpkin. On Christmas eve his great red stocking was hung on a nail outside his stall and filled with more vegetables, some lumps of sugar preceding them into the capacious toe. My sister Edith maintained that like the ass in Bethlehem he knelt on the stroke of midnight; but we were never allowed to stay up late enough to confirm her faith.

He lived to the ripe age of twenty-three. Long after we older children had gone away to school and he had become too weak in the knees to draw the

younger, he browsed at will among the hummocks of
Constancy's pasture. Her he outlived by several
years. My father could not tolerate the idea of has-
tening his final departure, and he died a natural
death.

Of all our family retainers he was the best loved.
I wish, indeed, that I could be as sure of gladness
upon the sight in the next world of people I have
known as I can be of my eager reunion with Richard.
And I trust that among the flora which populate the
"gardens and the goodly walks" of the New Jerusalem, there are numbered illimitable acres of carrots!

CHAPTER VI

GAMES AND PASTIMES

(1)

THE eighties and the nineties, indeed, even the first decade of the nineteen hundreds, did not encourage among average families the accumulation of mere things. In the first place, relatively simple means necessitated a lower standard of living; in the second, many people still believed and practised the wholesome doctrine that a man's life consisteth not in the abundance of his possessions. At Christmas we, in common with our contemporaries, were more likely to receive renovated gifts than many new ones. Dolls were born again by new wigs, replaced eyes, and fresh wardrobes; their buggies were painted and equipped with new blankets; cape-racers, those invincible sleds native to the State of Maine, were furnished with new rungs and runners. This principle of renovation, however, could hardly extend to games such as tiddlywinks, checkers, and lotto. To be sure, anagrams were sometimes cleverly restored; but for the most part games once gone were lost forever. We treasured them, therefore, for they were none too frequently seen in their bright pasteboard boxes either on birthdays or at Christmas

Of all these indoor pleasures the most popular was unquestionably the game of Authors. This priceless invention whiled away many a rainy afternoon. It is impossible, indeed, to overestimate its intellectual and cultural value. Children whose homes were far less addicted to books than was our own learned to recognize upon sight the faces of great men and women. They knew, too, by name at least their mighty works. Although Thomas Carlyle might never be read, the fact gleaned from one small card that he wrote *The French Revolution, Frederick the Great, Sartor Resartus,* and *Heroes and Hero Worship* was forever lodged in thousands of heads throughout the country. Today I am informed and have myself sadly corroborated the information that the modern game of Authors has been brought up to date by the inclusion of men and women of lesser stature, that Ralph Waldo Emerson, whose long, benign face we well knew, and George Eliot, whose brooch and parted hair we regarded with polite respect, have given place to Mr. Zane Grey and Mrs. Kathleen Norris. But we were acquainted with no such desecration. Even though our knowledge were not to extend beyond those bits of cardboard, we bandied about in common conversation names and books of renown.

"Have you *Daniel Deronda?*"

"Have you *In Memoriam?*"

"Have you *A Comedy of Errors?*"

Games of "cards" were still frowned upon by

many in our neighbourhood and elsewhere. My
grandmother always went sedately to bed when my
father began to shuffle our one dog-eared pack. He
felt that whist trained our powers of decision and
quick thinking, and on rare evenings when our lessons were learned he condescended to lay his book
aside and to play with us. Bridge of any denomina-
tion was unknown; and my father considered five
hundred and fan-tan lesser sports, beneath the dignity of his intelligence.

On Sundays the only games permitted us were the
Bible games. These two boxes, filled with bits of
green cardboard, one labelled *Old Testament*, the
other *New*, we had had in the family long before I
can remember. Although they were designed for
Sabbath profit, as the directions on the covers specifically stated, they were fully as exciting as any week-
day games. My father delighted in them, for they
gave him opportunity to show his wide and accurate
knowledge. He was always the Teacher provided for
in the rules, although it is but fair to say that he
never consulted the pink pamphlet assigned to his
position. We sat around him, my mother and grandmother usually joining us. Each player asked in turn
of the neighbour on his right the question on one of
the green cards dealt out to him at the beginning or
demanded that he fulfil the command given thereon:

"Where were the disciples first called Christians?"

"Name the twelve Apostles as they are recorded in
Matthew's gospel."

"Who were the two sons of the wise King Solomon?"

"Quote the exact words of the spirit of Samuel when it was disturbed by the thoughtless and wicked Witch of Endor."

"Name and spell correctly the three daughters of Job."

If the one questioned could not answer with exactness, the chance was given to the next on the right who through his correct answer claimed the card; if all failed, and even the slightest deviation in the case of quoted material constituted a failure, the card went to my father. Not once referring to the pink book, he gave the answer, we repeating it after him providing it were of any length or difficulty, like the triumphant song of Deborah, of which five verses were required, or the first ten verses of the Sermon on the Mount. After the game had been played and the green cards won by the successful, he asked in turn those which he had accumulated by our failures and presented them to those who had best profited by his instructions.

Of indoor games, not contained in boxes but rather dependent upon our own inventiveness, we had many. Charades were extraordinarily popular; and we were fortunate in being able to recruit our actors from the family, especially during vacation evenings when reading palled and when friends were in their own homes. We used to ponder over the dictionary during odd half hours or when we should have been dusting, in order to find rare words of many syllables which would act out well. My sister Edith, two years my junior and of a most versatile imagination, conceived a game based on our study of history. Under her supervision we enacted scenes which the others of the family were to guess. We made up in dramatic fervour what we lacked in properties. Thus she herself in a three-cornered hat framed from a newspaper, a broomstick in one hand, her feet in the baby's bath-tub, and untold determination on her face was Washington Crossing the Delaware!

Of spelling-bees we never tired, much as we were used to them in school. Here again our large family made other participants unnecessary. We utilized the servant in the kitchen to call out the words; and to the credit of average State of Maine intelligence be it said that even she did not too often have to con the speller over assiduously. Very rarely on Sundays we were allowed a spelling-bee in place of the Bible game; but on that day it was distinctly understood that the Scriptures alone should supply the words. Then *Zerubbabel* procured many a downfall as did *Jehoshaphat* and *Nebuchadnezzar*.

(2)

Our outdoor games were, I find, for the most part common to all children of our generation and doubtless to those of preceding and following. The most active games change surprisingly little from one era to another. Aside from those in which our various animals co-operated (for we could stage a reputable circus on very short notice!) we played the old games of tag, prisoner's base, and hide and seek. "London Bridge is Falling Down" was a favourite as was likewise another based also upon an old song, which inquiry leads me to think less familiar. It had a lovely lilting refrain:

> Round about the mulberry bush,
> John of Canterbury, O!

Uneventful as was the game itself, for it savoured of drop-the-handkerchief with even the handkerchief left out, it was a prime favourite probably because of its odd words, which made in our minds no real sense, and its airy, buoyant tune.

During the long summer evenings until our bedtime at eight or eighty-thirty we played with others of the neighbourhood in all manner of merrymakings, usually the noisier the better. But there was one diversion which never palled, serious and silent as it was by contrast. This was the making of ourselves into *statues*. A judge was chosen, usually by counting out, and he thereupon at once retired from the scene while we decided by individuals or by groups what we should personify. The odd thing about this amusement lay in its abstract nature. There was nothing to prevent our choosing to make our forms and our faces into images of well-known persons or representative of famous events. Rather we decided to typify various emotions or states of mind—Joy, Fear,

Pity, Hatred, Jealousy, Faith, Rage, Pride, Cruelty, Melancholy, and Grief. Sometimes one strove singly to make oneself into the outward and visible sign of some mental or spiritual mood; sometimes we functioned in small groups, our aim to present an ensemble like the Niobe in one of our history books. When we had finally decided what we were to represent, for which task we were allowed but a few minutes, we communicated this information to the judge, who if material was at hand wrote down the emotion or the state of mind opposite the name of the actor. If no pencil, paper, or slate were easily procurable, the judge relinquished his position in favour of mere guesswork.

Whence this game sprang it is impossible to say. Perhaps, indeed, it was born from gazing upon the reproductions of famous statuary in school-books. It seems to have been of relatively new growth; my mother had never played it. But it was dear to the children of my generation and environment. We always entered upon it with high seriousness, perhaps vaguely realizing that the emotions and the passions we attempted to portray were the very stuff and pattern of human life. Melancholy, clasping his knees, his head sunk upon his flannel blouse, remained for long, solemn minutes while the judge criticized, appraised, or attempted to guess what his posture indicated; Faith, gazing heavenward in a blue gingham apron, was too rapt in her contemplation of eternal verities to laugh; Jealousy, called to bed in the very act of stabbing his rival, preferred to incur punishment rather than to abandon his studied, awful formation until all chance of getting first place had been well lost.

(3)

Chief among our outdoor games was one which because of its great popularity and its rather original character deserves a space by itself. This was "Playing Pliny." I think it must have arisen among us from a favourite description in a school Reader of the death of Pliny the Elder from the eruption of Mount Vesuvius. Certain it is that it knew no equal in our affections between the ages of eight and thirteen.

One of the delightful features of this game lay in the exhaustive preparation which it required; another in the large number of children which it needed for complete effectiveness. On the mornings when we decided to play it, we gathered together all the available participants, the more the better. The first step was the collecting of stones. These we gathered, each for himself, in some receptacle which allowed of hasty expulsion. We had a high sense of honour about the size of the stones; they must be neither too large nor too sharp. At least an hour was needed before enough had been found for a really successful game.

The stones gathered, Pliny was chosen. His was too great a distinction to be lightly allotted by the familiar method of counting out. Instead, slips of paper were prepared, upon one of which was printed

P-L-I-N-Y,

well shaken together, and drawn carefully one by one
from a cap or hat. Once chosen, Pliny withdrew to
the barn to prepare himself (or herself) for the
awful eruption and for his subsequent death by falling stones and lava. His preparation consisted of pro-
curing a slate and pencil and of covering his back,
shoulders, and head with a very large pillow. My
mother in some odd and generous hour had made the
pillow expressly for this game from a discarded
feather tick and had fashioned also broad bands to
secure it around Pliny's neck and breast.

Meanwhile Vesuvius prepared to do its utmost!
A certain narrow avenue of apple trees in our orchard
constituted the favourite scene of action since it was
possible, as Pliny made his tortuous way between
them, for us from our perches in the branches to
shower our stones upon him in a truly realistic manner.

Even today my nerves tingle at the remembrance
of that game of games. I see Pliny stoically endeav-
ouring at the outset to note upon his slate the unnatural phenomena of sky and sea, only an occasional
shower of stones quickening his anxiety; I see him
shortly, staggering beneath the ever-increasing rain
from an unkind heaven, his progress each moment
becoming more desperate. I hear his stifled groans
resounding through the orchard (for we had gathered from the Reader that he was a restrained as well

as a noble Roman!). I still witness the failure of his heavy feet, his lonely death beneath his pillow!

Of this game we never tired. We even paid without much remonstrance a high price for it. For my father, although he encouraged its playing, insisted that at least the larger stones be found among the grass before the scythes of the hay-men in July should be dulled by them. He was wise enough, however, not to insist upon our picking them up after each performance; and thus we played on with no dull aftermath to obscure the awful tragedy.

It is safe to say that to at least half the participants this game constituted their sole venturing among the classics. But that even the name of Pliny thereby remains secure in the minds of ten middle-aged persons justifies the pastime among us. As for myself, I am convinced that from it was born my affection both for the *Natural History* of the Elder and the *Letters* of the Younger, an affection immeasurably enhanced by the knowledge that I once partook with all my heart in the tragic activities of their noble family.

(4)

As for pastimes not included under the name of games we had many and delightful ones, uneventful as they may seem today. Only the most cherished can be recorded here, nor can here be described those which arose from the nearness of the sea and which will be treated in another chapter. In March with my father's help we tapped the nearby maples, inserting

tin spouts beneath his auger holes and watching day
by day the sap dripping slowly into pails, later to be
boiled into syrup by my good-natured mother and
eaten on piles of flap-jacks. In the spring, too, we
plunged our bared arms into icy pools after jellied
masses of frogs' eggs and placed them in fruit-jars to
develop under our eager scrutiny into tadpoles.
When these, like Jeshurun, waxed fat and kicked, re-
belling against their narrow quarters, we carried
them to the wider liberties of the pasture brook and
left them free to continue their sensational evolution
into frogs. In the summer we picked berries, that desultory occupation which could never rightly be
termed labour in those days before the advent of
blueberry rakes. We crouched among the juniper
and ferns on the high uplands, filling our pails in no
great haste and gazing out to sea whenever we liked.
In the long winter afternoons, when it was too cold
or wet for coasting or skating, we popped corn, shaping its puffed kernels with the addition of boiled
molasses into great circular balls, one of which with
judicious chewing would last an ecstatic hour.

And always there was reading. That, after all, was
our most treasured indoor pastime. Each of us had
a favourite corner in the library or the living-room,
and there we crouched for hours, when we were not
needed in the care of the younger children, lost in
the Scottish Highlands or in David Copperfield's
London until a painful cramp in our shoulders or the
clock striking the hour for some chore brought us to

our senses. My mother somehow found time for reading to us, although how she did it remains a mystery. She liked to choose books which all of us from sixteen to six could enjoy, and she had her own opinions as to the titles of these. One was Lamb's *Tales from Shakespeare;* another, *The Swiss Family Robinson;* a third, the poems of Whittier, especially *The Swan Song of Parson Avery.* When she read for an hour in the evening, my father always listened with us, the book mattering little to him.

There were parties, of course, but only occasionally. Evening ones were especially rare, and for us they terminated early, for my father invariably appeared to fetch us at quarter to nine, in the winter the light from his lantern swinging threateningly across the snow just as the refreshments were being served. We never heard of dancing-school, dancing even in the nineties in such communities as ours being considered unwise if not actually immoral. For children it was unheard of. Needless to say, motion pictures were unknown, and the nearest theatre of any sort was thirty miles away. To be sure, once during the summer a travelling show usually appeared, playing *Uncle Tom's Cabin* or *East Lynne.* But harmless as was the nature of the production, to which children were almost never taken, the producers were looked upon with suspicion by the best people, and a corporate sigh of relief marked their departure.

All in all, our games and our pastimes were enjoyed at home and among ourselves. My mother, although she now and then allowed us the excitement of "spending the day" with a friend or an afternoon with a neighbour, had small patience with a reiterant desire to "go somewhere." "A gadder," she was forever saying, "comes to grief." Our evenings were inevitably spent at home, in winter with our reading or our lessons, in summer with our outdoor pleasures. During vacation in the winter she or my father often proposed the holding of what we called a family concert, though the name was a misnomer as we were all notoriously unmusical. This affair, for which we made programs, was staged in the kitchen after the supper dishes were washed and consisted of a recitation by each of us, the audience our long-suffering parents and those who were not at the moment performing. Bedtimes were rigid and unchangeable: For those just emerged from babyhood, seven o'clock; for the half-sized, eight in winter, eight-thirty in summer; for all in their teens, nine.

One evening when I was twelve I came home at an unprecedented hour. The occasion, which must have been momentous, I forget; but I shall never forget the hands of the clock on the dining-room mantel. They pointed to twenty minutes to ten, a position in which I had never before beheld them at night! To me they connoted a mysterious depth of experience which I can find no words to describe; and I have never forgotten the awe with which I regarded them.

CHAPTER VII

WAYFARING LIFE IN THE NINETIES

(1)

"NOT many sounds in life," wrote Charles Lamb, "and I include all rural and urban sounds, exceed in interest a knock at the door." Doubtless the assertion was true, in his day and at *his* door; but in the year 1932 it is open to grave question at any door at all. Too often a hasty glance at the automobile outside tells us whom to expect before we have turned the latch. Or we may hastily surmise with good reason that it is just another boy putting himself through college on magazine subscriptions or just another nondescript man putting himself through life by exhibiting a vacuum cleaner. Sometimes, of course, even now the unexpected happens. The wife of the president of one of our colleges recently delighted me by telling of one of these larger guerdons of Fortune. She opened her door not long ago to be greeted without initial ceremony by a gentleman who said blithely, "Good morning! Now speaking of vanilla!" And I myself had recently the inestimable luck of finding on my threshold a tense lady in a strange hat, who cried by way of in-

74

troducing herself and her mission, "Madam, do you believe in God, Jesus, and the Bible?"

But such treasured exceptions at best are rare. Easy transit does not encourage wayfaring on foot; and easy prosperity has dictated that too few of us respond in person to the knocks and rings at our own doors. Hence it is that even rural children today cannot know the excitement which was ours in the nineties when every summer brought its slow and patient travellers.

Chief among these, at least in corporate interest and concern, were gypsies. Why these nomads chose our hostile countryside can be explained only by their inexplicable selves. Certain it is that they were more unwelcome than an August drought. They were viewed with suspicion as thieves, with hatred as idlers and ne'er-do-wells, and with fear as purveyors of the grossest superstitions as well as the most awful diseases. Once the frightened, fascinated children in the straggling houses along our road had given warning of their approach by running breathless to every back door and thereby recruiting themselves substantially, close-lipped housewives hastened to pull the front shades, to lock all doors, and to gather as successfully as they could all their scattered children beneath their wings.

Then, from behind the curtains of darkened rooms, from the open windows of hay-lofts, from the tops of apple trees we watched them pass. Not a detail escaped us: their mangy, rickety horses; their dishevelled covered wagons, creaking and rumbling through the summer dust; their short, laughing men, dark, kerchiefed women, and dirty, sniffling, barefoot children; the pails swinging from their axle-trees; the babel of an unfamiliar tongue. Secretly we loved the captivating confusion which they not only possessed but engendered. We clung tenaciously to the hope that a certain family on the outskirts of the village and itself in ill-repute among us would not deny them a camping-place. For we knew that in spite of the bitterness accorded them by all our God-fearing elders, they would, once established, insinuate themselves into our yards, knock at our closed doors, beg to tell our fortunes, until they should be summarily ordered from the premises by the heads of homes, who not infrequently stayed away from business for that very necessity.

We knew, too, that even our elders could not restrain their curiosity once the gypsies had lighted their evening fires. Sometimes certain of our fathers, weighted by the responsibility of preserving order and decency in the community, felt it incumbent upon them to watch these nomadic proceedings from a respectable distance; sometimes—oh, rare and happy occasions!—they took us with them while they made their reconnoitrings. And although they instructed us well concerning the sloth and sin of the strangers within our outermost gates, they could not dull our delighted imaginations. These kept us awake at night and aroused us betimes in the morning. For we knew full well that some hen-yard in town in spite of their surveillance would find itself depleted in fowls but enhanced in importance. At such times we ourselves envied those whose parents kept hens and chickens, knowing that the gypsies would not attempt any raids upon the more substantial beasts in our stable. Nevertheless, on the night they tarried near us we barricaded the door of the barn with a great joist and brought indoors all our lesser creatures. All in all, with doubtful thanks to the supervision of our parents, I suppose we gathered less first-hand information about gypsies than we gleaned at second-hand from Maggie Tulliver, who was in our school Reader as well as in our own library. But the thrills which attended their welcome approach still linger on, to the extent, indeed, that should I see their Ford cars drawing near my home, even in the ample town where I now reside, I am sure I should revert to type, immediately draw my front shades, and bolt my doors.

(2)

Indians were far more hospitably received. They were a trifle less dirty for one thing, and for another they usually approached us singly or at worst in pairs. Moreover, there was a tacit feeling among us that they were more native than foreign. They came from their colony at Oldtown on the Penobscot or from Eastport on Passamaquoddy. There was a certain dignity about the lanky stride of the men, the taciturn, high-boned faces of the women. On rare occasions my mother bought a sweet-grass basket from them, seeing therein an inexpensive and unusual Christmas gift for some urban friend or relative. My father liked to talk with them concerning their communal life although I think he was always a bit disappointed in their lack of response to his comments on their stirring history.

Sometimes instead of baskets they sold medicines, various salves and tonics. In the disposal of these I think they were more successful. Baskets were after all luxuries, whereas a beneficial mixture, made exclusively as they always averred from the herbs of the fields and tested as to its efficacy upon any number of Indians, might prove in the long run less dear than even infrequent doctor's bills. Moreover, since the nature of man is ever to seek release from major or minor bodily ills and likewise seldom to be averse to the delineation of them, these wandering herbalists did no little business especially among the outlying districts.

My mother stoutly set her face against their remedies. She felt that we, as more enlightened town dwellers, should not be led away by them. But my father grievously disappointed her by purchasing each spring from a very tall and old Indian, who claimed to be a Penobscot chief, a great bottle labelled "Kickapoo Indian Sagwaw." This concoction, which was black and syrupy, emitted a really delectable smell. With each yearly acquisition my father alternately sniffed the contents and read the ingredients, which with commendable if not complete honesty were printed upon the label beneath the feathered head of an Indian chief.

"Horehound, anise, checkerberry, sarsaparilla, camomile, wormwood"—thus he would enumerate to my mother as he laughed at her misgivings. "Herbs made for the service of man."

But she remained obdurate until three unopened bottles had collected on the shelf in the cellarway. What influence finally proved her undoing, I do not know. Perhaps it was her innate thrift, for my father's relative extravagance caused her no little anxiety. At all events, one March morning she began to alternate the Sagwaw with the sulphur and molasses, which with the coming of spring was always dealt out to us on the principle of three mornings in succession following by a skipping of the three ensuing.

This consumption of sulphur and molasses was a rite familiar to rural New England and needs neither introduction nor description to middle-aged and elderly New England readers. The two ingredients were mixed in a large bowl to the consistency of a heavy paste. In our large family we ranged ourselves before breakfast in a line and received, each from the same big spoon, a mouthful, which in the phraseology of today would be termed "capacity." The taste was not unpleasant, although the double nature of the dose sometimes made swallowing a long and complicated process. Much easier and more agreeable in every way was the Sagwaw, which, though it was perhaps a trifle bitter, savoured of spring woods and disappeared with ease.

Whether we received any benefits from either of these tonics beyond the sense of family solidarity which they engendered I cannot say. Certain it is that we received no harm. I am sure, too, that my nephews and nieces, who are beset by baby specialists, carrots, orange juice, and spinach, present no better appearance of health than did we in our day. It is at least a matter of some regret that they will never know that family rite, instituted by sulphur and molasses, alleviated by Kickapoo Indian Sagwaw, and carrying in its long wake such resultant humour in reminiscence.

(3)

There were other wanderers among us, less exciting at the time of their appearance but pleasant to look back upon. Scissors grinders plied a busy trade whenever they wheeled or carried their heavy circular stones down any of the four roads which brought them into Blue Hill. The minor tones of their bells sound often in my ears like the muted notes of those ancient sheep-bells still to be heard among the highlands of Scotland and not infrequently found in London junk-shops and on the stands of rural English market-places. They did a respectable job and were treated with respect although no one inquired as to whence they came or whither they were going. To

us children, although we procured the necessary pail
of water and watched with eagerness the silvery dust
arising from the dull knives or the scissors blades as
they met the turning stone, they possessed no especial
romance other than that provided by any stranger
within our circumscribed midst.

Less intriguing even than they were certain zealous souls who now and again knocked at our doors.
These labourers in the vineyard were sometimes tem-
perance enthusiasts, sometimes travelling evangelists,
sometimes Mormons. I remember two of the last-
named who called upon us one noon when I was in
my early teens. Invited to dinner by my hospitable
father, who was moved by curiosity as well as by
kindness, they sat at our table and told us of Utah
and the Great Salt Lake which we knew only from
our geographies. They told us, too, of Brigham
Young and of Joseph Smith, of the sufferings endured by them and their followers in a wilderness of
mountains and sand. They were young men with
blazing eyes. The tenets of their faith meant nothing
to me, but the intensity of their devotion to it has
remained.

"God," said one of them, holding his tumbler in
a perilous position, "gave His earlier chosen people
water from Moses' smiting of a rock. To us, His
chosen people today, He gave courage to bring water
thirty-five miles from the hills to His new City!"

Tracts were in common circulation among us in the

early nineties. These were not infrequently brought to our doors by dusty men with valises from which they extricated their pamphlets, often with some pious injunction as to the profit we should gain therefrom. These wanderers had less appeal, even to my father, and we seldom invited them indoors. But I read their wares now and then when I longed for new reading matter. I remember one about a little girl named Martha who converted all her "large and careless family" by a self-imposed fast of three days. Led by the Spirit, this incredible child ate not a mouthful of food nor drank so much as "the smallest cup of cold water until her time should be fulfilled." I always thought of her on Saturday nights when the warm, comforting smell of baked beans and brown bread assailed my nostrils and tickled my stomach. To myself I said that her fast doubtless took place on Monday, Tuesday, and Wednesday. But even on those days I knew it would be useless for me to attempt emulation; and I felt relieved that my family, though surely large, could not be termed so "careless" as hers had been as to their immortal souls.

For several successive summers a tall thin man with a long beard called at our house. He was the purveyor of what he called "Comfort Powders." These were tiny bits of white paper, folded like medicinal powders. Opened, each revealed a verse of Scripture of a distinctly comforting nature. I remember him, perhaps not so much because of his quieting doses as because of my grandmother's terrible anger when one day we so far forgot ourselves as to laugh at him and to call out taunts behind his attenuated back. Our parents were away on their yearly vacation trip to Boston else we should never have ventured upon such self-expression; but my grandmother's punishment was singularly effective. Calling us into the house, she read to us in a threatening, awful voice that just tale of the children who laughed at the Prophet Elisha, calling him Baldhead. The summary destruction of forty and two of them by two she-bears from the woods remained with us long as a wholesome deterrent against disrespect for the aged.

(4)

But ever we took the greatest delight in the Oriental pedlars who came among us once the roads had dried in the spring. These were for the most part Armenian or Syrian women of middle age, travelling alone with a huge oil-cloth-covered pack on each hip. They wore red handkerchiefs over their black hair, ear-rings, and necklaces of bright stones. To us children they were the epitome of all that was strange, outlandish, and romantic.

That the reserve and suspicion native to the rural New Englander tolerated these foreigners is singular. It is more singular still that in many cases they were actually welcome among us. Perhaps some hang-over from seafaring days, when the dark faces of men from Barbados and Martinique were no uncommon sight, lingered. Perhaps the economics of the countryside dictated their reception; for they invariably carried, in addition to their embroideries for the few wealthy summer residents here and there, the ordinary necessities for family-sewing-baskets often far from any other source of supply. Perhaps they themselves ensured friendliness as their natural right, attracting it by their Oriental dignity and courtesy and holding it by some gift or gifts within themselves.

Surely this last was true in the case of one who traversed Maine seacoast villages for twenty years. Her name was Mary Christmas. She was a Syrian, whose husband had been massacred by the Turks. The coast road from Kittery to Eastport as well as many outlying roads therefrom knew her well; and it is safe to say there is not a village which does not even now remember her with gratitude.

She was a beautiful woman, large and tall with a mobile, olive face and great glowing eyes. Her nature, too, was large and bountiful, her energy tireless, almost overwhelming. She would walk with her heavy pack for miles along country roads sometimes in a drenching rain, to be given at nightfall the grudging offer at a farmhouse of the hay-loft for the night. More often than not after ten minutes' conversation she would find herself in the spare room. Her stories of her far-off country became a cherished property of hundreds of Maine children; and the contents of her mysterious bundles were cheerfully shown to those who had no intention to purchase.

My own family was especially happy in its long association with Mary Christmas. She came into our village when I was ten. Accused of an attempt to defraud some shrewd housewife of change, she was brought before my father who at once befriended and acquitted her. She was thereafter our friend and our guest for whom yearly we watched and waited.

It is impossible to rehearse or to over-estimate all that she did for us. Her ambitions for her children across the seas fired us with larger thoughts for ourselves; the buoyancy of her feet and of her imagination made us less weary in our smaller adventures in well-doing; the concrete beauty and drama of her older religious faith, her tales of saints and of wonder-working relics, one of which she wore around her neck, lent colour and elasticity to the unyielding and inflexible theology of our early years. We saw her advance in sufficient prosperity to abandon her black packs for a stout push-cart with red wheels; we witnessed the bringing of her children to America.

In 1904 she died, following an operation in a Bangor hospital. In the same city her son and her grandson now carry on her trade in Syrian laces and embroideries. They have in their faces much of the nobility of her own. In their pride in her memory they are upheld by thousands of Maine seacoast people who knew and honoured her. She held first place among all the wayfarers who brightened the more remote communities of the nineties, and it will be long before she is forgotten among them.

CHAPTER VIII

RELATIVES ACTUAL OR ASSUMED

(1)

OUR family was unique among families in Blue
Hill in that we had few near relatives. My
mother had been an only child; of my father's three
sisters two had died young, one lived elsewhere. To
be sure we were united to the population at large by
several different strands; few, in fact, of the three
hundred households which made the village and its
environs were unconnected with one another through
some line. But such intermarriage, though it may figure large in the cogitations of the sociologist, did not
constitute relationship to us. In town we had no actual aunts and uncles whom we knew and no cousins
near at hand.

In Quincy, Massachusetts, however, lived two
relatives whose yearly visits and whose somewhat
portentous gifts throughout the year played a large
part in our lives and thoughts. These were my
father's aunt, our great-aunt Maria, and her husband,
great-uncle John. Every August they arrived on the
Boston boat to spend an exciting fortnight in our
home. Aunt Maria was a handsome woman whose
slender income never betrayed itself in her careful

appearance and dignified manner. She favoured especially black satin or taffeta in her costumes, and one was always conscious of some fine bit of white material which lent just the proper finish in the shape of a vest, a collar, or a bow at her neck. These accoutrements of her dress seemed inexhaustible; the same gown might be worn from day to day, but its finishing touch was always so new and interesting as to excite comments—comments, I may add, which with all her volubility she rarely regarded.

Uncle John was a tall, bald old man with furious moustaches like Lewis Carroll's walrus. He always carried his hands clasped behind his back and said, "Well! Well!" in heated ejaculations whether there was anything to be heated about or not. Perhaps he had been consigned to ejaculations years earlier by his wife's tendency to talk. She was an indefatigable conversationalist, speaking rapidly and with many questions. These were mostly rhetorical, nothing whatever depending upon the answers to them. They were generous souls, never appearing without gifts for each and every member of the family. But it was their gifts during the remainder of the year which, at least in retrospect, caused such commotion among us.

These donations were made possible partly through the native munificence of Uncle John, partly by reason of the business in which he was engaged. He was the travelling representative of a casket firm in Washington, D. C. It is but fair to say that this rather sombre business sat lightly upon him; indeed, he expatiated to my father upon the economics which underlay the rise and fall of his merchandise in precisely the tone one might have employed for less significant commodities like potatoes or eggs. He pointed out with many ejaculations what slaves persons were in death as in life to fashions and what exigencies he and his firm were likely to suffer by such mortuary waves. We children, completely fascinated by this strange conversation, sat stiff and silent in a row on the porch steps during his recitals.

Upon these occasions my mother was always torn between her double duty as a parent and a hostess. She was doomed also to other periods of indecision when now and again during the year a large box arrived from Uncle John's Washington firm. This contained divers samples of coffin-linings in silks, satins and laces, not only in white but in truly delectable shades of cream, lavender, mauve, grey and purple. Each sample was in size some twelve inches square and could easily suggest to my mother's practical eye a dozen possible uses.

We children were supposed to remain in ignorance as to the intrinsic nature of these bits of material, the employment for which they had been fashioned. But after an ill-timed and facetious remark of my father had shattered that possibility, my mother saw that there was nothing for it but to lay all cards on the table. Thereupon ensued a family consultation in which the older children participated. On the one hand, there were the generosity of our relatives, the inherent usefulness of their gifts to us, and the sensible knowledge that so far as *we* were concerned there was not the slightest relation in these fabrics to anything strange or queer; on the other, there existed at most only a nonsensical notion which bore no weight at all in the face of plain common sense. It will be at once evident that the yeas entirely overbalanced the one feeble nay! The coffin-linings were, therefore, utilized to their fullest extent over a period of years, my mother cautioning us, however, against the need or the advisability of informing the curious as to what they were or whence they came.

They were in truth put to manifold uses. Two in white satin of the same likeness would fashion a charming baby's bonnet; two more in lace, a guimpe for a summer dress. Our wide leghorn hats were summer by summer refurbished by new rosettes and bands in shades at which our envious associates marvelled. The coloured bits were employed also for pipings or for covering buttons or for edging small comforters and blankets. My mother, quick to seize upon the ingenuity of Aunt Maria, freshened up her none too plentiful wardrobe by a frill here, a bow there. Our dolls were the best dressed in the neighbourhood. At Christmas we gave at no expense whatever the most engaging sachets and pin-cushions to our friends.

In those years we might well have been approved by the prophet, for although I cannot say we went "softly," we often carried about with us suggestions of another world! To that world Aunt Maria and Uncle John have long since passed. Large and bountiful be their reward! For they provided our childhood with the exciting gifts of contrivance and of secrecy and our maturer years with a source of unextinguishable laughter.

(2)

My mother had a step-sister whom we called Do, pronouncing her name not like the verb of action but like the female of the deer family. She was not native to Blue Hill but through girlhood association with my mother had married there. Her husband was the village postmaster. Childless herself, she knew no limits in her generosity to us, and we adored her. In those days of shawls, which during the winter months swathed most women from shoulders to ankles, she wore one of tan camel's hair with long fringe, and she invariably secreted within its elbowed crevices cookies, home made candies, and cup-cakes. Her regular Saturday afternoon visits ensured my mother against our begging to "go somewhere."

Her gifts to us were tangible and substantial like herself. Chief among them was her bi-yearly invitation to spend the day in her square red brick house beyond a cedar-lined driveway and within but a few feet of the water of the bay. Especially satisfying were these invitations because our parents were never included in them. We went by ourselves, well-brushed and scrubbed, in clean blouses or in clean aprons over our woollen dresses. We went at nine in the morning, and we came home at supper-time. This long, corporate absence from home under Do's very lenient supervision early gave rise not only to the tacit understanding that for two days in the three hundred and sixty-five we were free to do precisely as we pleased but also to the equally tacit agreement that we divulge at night no unnecessary detail. Although like all other children we might "tell on" one another on lesser days, our loyalty, one to all and all to one, on these occasions was complete.

Three memorable features mark these visits. The first, in fact, governed the seasons in which the days occurred. For we were asked to Do's for the express purpose of eating all we could possibly contain of a certain food; and late spring and summer were adjudged, even in days less given to caution in matters of diet, as unwise for this particular consumption. Hence our days with her usually occurred in late fall and in early spring when time was apt to drag a bit and when some stimulant was not unwelcome.

The stimulant provided by Do in addition to others of a less concrete nature was a superabundant supply of potato chips. These toothsome, curving disks, brown, transparent, and salt-flaked, were not thirty years ago procurable in a well-lined package at ten cents from any grocery store. They were instead a rarity, and the making of them was dependent upon the possession of a certain instrument designed for the purpose. Do was the sole woman in town with a chip-slicer. When she screwed this to her kitchen table, placed therein a potato well peeled and washed, pressed upon it with her fingers to keep it in the right position, and turned a tiny crank, the potato came from its circular mouth reduced to the thinnest slivers. These then were dropped into a cauldron of hissing fat, only a second later to be lifted, transformed, into pans covered with brown paper.

Now potatoes were not in the nineties a subject of intense social agitation. That they contained abundant calories no one was aware, just as no one was aware of those ticketed and alphabetized vitamins which presumably then as now invisibly quickened the life of certain vegetables and fruits. Ninety-nine families out of a hundred would have stared, incredulous, at a potato-less dinner; indeed, a large proportion of them ate potatoes for supper and for breakfast as well. With this in mind or in memory both Do and my mother must remain blameless for the doubtless sinister condition of our stomachs at the conclusion of our bi-yearly repast.

Of course, it is but fair to the latter to state that she was in complete ignorance as to the number of chips we consumed. It was the one occasion of our youthful lives when no check was put upon us; and, secure in the knowledge of Do's ideals as a hostess, we knew that she could be no source of information. We ate literally until we could hold no more. Indeed, when we at last pushed our chairs from the table, gorged and stuffed with so much potato that

we had with difficulty found space for a triangle of
hot and excellent apple pie, each might well have
cried with Pepys, "My dinner was noble and
enough!" I must believe that good digestion in those
days waited on our unseemly appetites; for I recall
but few instances when Do administered the essence
of peppermint which she was never without; and although today I eschew potatoes in all forms, I cannot
forget the sense of well-being which I possessed
when I arose from that depleted board.

Our minds, too, were fed at Do's and those, also,
in an equally reckless and delightful manner. In her
parlour she possessed a huge and ungainly book, the
second feature of our days with her. This volume,
which measured two feet by one and a half, was a
compendium of horrors. It had no title. We called it
from its colour the *Green Book*. A globe outlined
with all its continents in gold adorned its cover.
Within, its great pages contained harrowing accounts
of the most terrifying incidents known on land or sea.
We used to spread it open upon the floor and lie before it on our distended stomachs while one of us
read aloud to the others its desperate, stirring contents and all gazed upon its shocking and ghastly
pictures.

Space forbids me to recount even our favourites.
The annals of the dire ravages of yellow fever in the
Carolinas; the minute relation of the catastrophes attendant upon the Johnstown flood; the calamitous
effects upon the children of a town in Texas when a

ghost appeared in a darkened school-room; the swallowing of a black boy by a boa-constrictor on the Amazon; the multitudinous horrors following hard upon a cyclone in a far western territory—all these strove for supremacy with one another. While Do washed the dinner dishes, for here again her generosity allowed of no assistance, we stored up our minds against dull hours and counted our own thin lives uneventful enough.

As for me, these days had yet a third feature. While the others, exhausted at length by an excess of tragedies, decided to play with the more unfamiliar set of neighbourhood children (for our own house was nearly a mile from Do's) I turned to yet another book which I knew only on these beneficent days. This was Marie Corelli's *Thelma*. I never asked to borrow it, feeling instinctively certain that my father would find it wanting in comparison with those I read at home; but I revelled in it on two afternoons of every year. Its midnight, "without darkness and without stars," its dwarf of fearsome aspect but benevolent mind, its impassioned love scenes, its high yet wicked society, all remained with me long after I had returned to the slower narratives of Creasy and of Waverley.

To dietitians, professional "educators," and psychoanalysts, had they then existed in such competent authority, we should have presented a sad picture as we trailed homeward at supper-time, our lips loyally sealed as to certain details of our exhilarating day.

But I have no cause to regret those festivals provided by Do. I hope, indeed, that she may read this late appreciation of herself and of her gifts, gleaning therefrom some apprehension of our corporate thanksgiving.

(3)

Another relative, more "assumed" even than Do, for she possessed no ties of kindred even by marriage, was my "Aunt" Caroline. I use the singular pronoun advisedly, for I think she perhaps meant more to me in my formative years than she meant to my brothers and sisters. She lived near us in a gracious house with beautiful carvings over its inside doors and stately pillars without. She was a short, small woman, almost tiny, with remarkable eyes. They were grey and shone like those of a seer or a saint. She was herself both a seer and a saint; and her gifts, intangible, immaterial, unsubstantial, must not remain unchronicled.

I knew her from my earliest childhood until her death in my twenty-third year. My relationship with her was from the first no ordinary one. Although she was the neighbour of neighbours, always present in time of any need, I knew her, and like to remember her best, more in her spiritual capacity than in any other. I use the adjective here in its largest, most illimitable sense. Excellent housekeeper though she was, the quick performance of her tasks was always more a means to an end than any end in itself. The order and harmony of her house were necessary to the order and harmony of her mind and spirit. The two staring china dogs on her mantel faced one way and no other; the straight line of four yellow bowls on her pantry shelf deviated not an inch in their respective positions; the open Bible on her sitting-room table lay always at a certain angle. Yet one was never conscious of fussiness or over-precision, only of a gracious order.

Like every housewife of her generation and position she worked all the forenoon at something or other. She would have thought it unbecoming to sit down before she was "cleaned up" for the afternoon. But even as a child I knew she was no slave to her broom, her mixing-bowls, or her oven. Her very phraseology in regard to these necessary labours was proof of that. For when, on the excuse of helping, I received permission to spend an hour of the morning with her, she always assigned our separate tasks after a manner unknown to *our* kitchen:

"Now suppose you *kind of* dust the sitting-room while I *kind of* stir up this gingerbread, and then we'll *kind of* straighten up the cooking things together."

I loved those hours in the morning. Yet in looking back upon them I cannot discover any outstanding feature which made them vivid. I am sure they must have passed prosaically enough to the outward eye. But there was a spirit diffused from the sunlight on the yellow floor-boards of my Aunt Caroline's kitchen which was nowhere else and which lured me again and again to her side door under the syringa bushes. I know now that it was, in Pater's words, "that deep, effusive unction of the House of Bethany."

As I grew older and felt within me those uneasy stirrings of earliest adolescence, I found conversation more simple and natural here than elsewhere. I could be more unrestrained as to my vaulting, ever-changing ambitions. She was quite able to see me one day as the most capable of country doctors, driving on errands of mercy here and there about the countryside, and the next as a rising young author with the world at my feet. To her I could represent myself with impunity as a person with an important future, whereas at home my dreams were likely to be dimmed by the practical reminder that I was only one of seven and in all likelihood of no especial talent whatsoever. I read to her the bad stories I had written and the worse verses. It was in her kitchen and sitting-room that I first felt emboldened to essay new words which I was shy of using in the company of my contemporaries or even too frequently at home. *Monotonous* was one of these; another was *weird*; a third, *romantic*.

For years she was my Sunday-school teacher. Her knowledge of the Bible exceeded the minister's and even my father's and far outdistanced that of my eclectic grandmother. Every Sunday morning after the church service we gathered in the white pews at just the right-hand centre of the church. She stood in a pew in front of us in her black bonnet with velvet strings and her grey stuff dress with white ruching at the high neck. She transcended the heavy piety of the lessons we learned weekly from a dull pamphlet called *A Harvest for Young Christians*. Through her, Absalom became a pathetic rather than an arrogant young man and Saint Paul a celestial as well as a terrestrial adventurer. One had to study long and hard to satisfy her demands. In addition to the weekly lesson, we memorized a psalm or a given chapter, which must be recited perfectly with every word clearly enunciated and no intonation slurred or undervalued. During our recitals she stood before us, her glowing eyes now on the speaker, now on the sky through the high, clear windows, a tiny red spot burning on either cheek.

For years, too, she employed a custom which made its peculiar and lasting impression upon us. She used to ask the members of her class to come to see her on the last night of the year. During an hour or so we entertained ourselves with the simple diversions of the period, with playing games, popping corn, or boiling and pulling molasses candy. But the diversions have passed into oblivion in comparison with the high moment of the evening which occurred just before our departure.

The first of these indelible occasions took place when I was twelve years old in the year 1899. On that evening just before the clock said eight-thirty and our bed-times approached, she presented each one of us with a pencil and a slip of paper.

"Write," she commanded as she stood in our midst. "Write this date, 'December 31st, 1899.' You will never in this way write it again. A century has passed, and a new one is beginning!"

I can still feel the catch in my throat as my fingers obeyed her. The solemnity of her words and the intensity with which she spoke them engendered far more than fear. There was in them the mystery of the passing of laden centuries, the awfulness of time in relation to Timelessness, the littleness and unimportance of us all—things gigantic and intangible enough, yet dimly perceived in that quiet room. We carried the papers silently home with us, and year by year on successive Decembers we added another and yet another to them. Small wonder is it that to me, even today, that date is in Hazlitt's words "like 'the dreaded name of Demogorgon.' "

With the growing perception of the significance of this yearly act there came another and more overwhelming revelation: I began to understand that my Aunt Caroline loved God more than she feared Him. Perhaps the chapters which immediately follow and which attempt to delineate religion as we knew it thirty years ago may serve to explain the astounding nature of this discovery. Suffice it is to say that she was the only person I had ever known of whom this was true. The fear of God was our daily mental food. To love Him, not for the purpose of extorting something from Him here and now, not for a reward after death, but actually because He was worthy to be loved was well-nigh inconceivable. Yet my aunt loved Him for Himself alone. This fact was slowly borne in upon me in all its simple, beneficent Truth.

Years were required for the revulsion and renovation of my theological concepts; but a start was made in my early teens by my aunt's consuming love of God. While she lay through the long months of her last hideous illness, that stupendous assurance was hourly made manifest. When I had hurried home from the West to see her, wasted now to little more than a pair of shining eyes waiting in a great bed, I was reassured of its imperishable Reality.

She died, singularly yet fittingly enough, on the thirty-first day of December in the year 1910.

PART II

THE PURITAN TRADITION

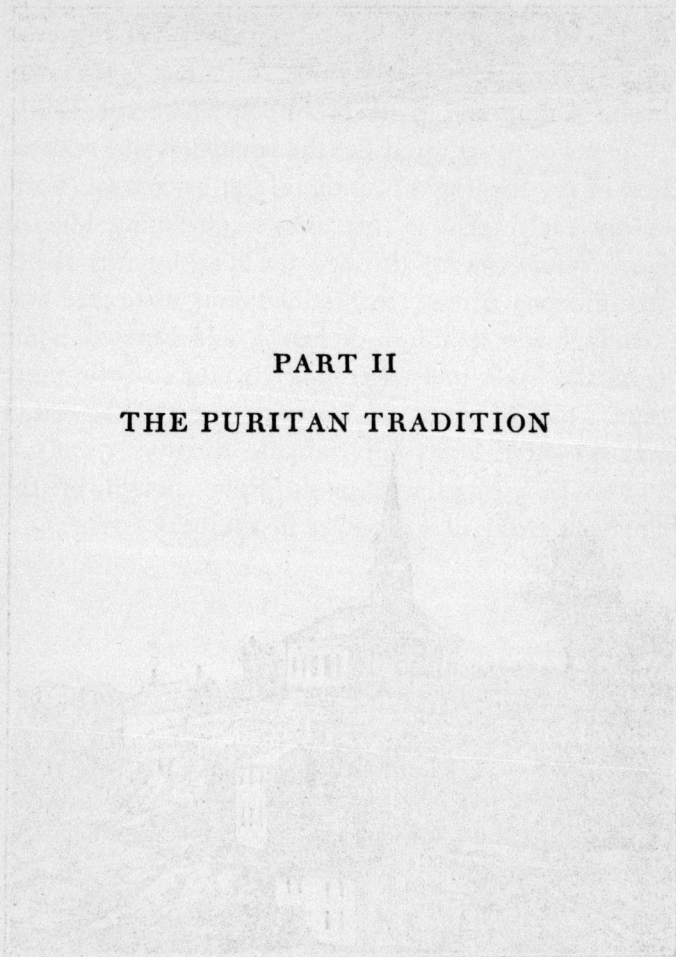

CHAPTER I

THE EARLY CHURCH IN BLUE HILL

(1)

ONE of the express conditions of the grant finally given by the General Court of Massachusetts to the early settlers of Blue Hill, including the two who squatted with no rights upon her shores, was "that they build in each Township a suitable Meeting-house for the public worship of God, and Settle a Learned Protestant Minister, and make Provision for his comfortable and honourable Support." Indeed, it was definitely stipulated that unless this condition should be fulfilled within six years of the date of the grant, 1762, all rights to the land should be forfeited by the proprietors and a fine might be in addition levied upon them.

Although as in other isolated and relatively unimportant communities early records of proceedings are scarce, there are existing documents to show that the first part of this agreement was punctiliously kept. Within a year or at most two after settlement a meeting-house was erected. The "Learned Protestant Minister," however, was not procured as a permanent resident for some thirty-seven years! The explanation of this neglect and evasion of responsibility was given in 1785 when the General Court, apparently careful even of its outlying grants and grantees, started an investigation, threatened forfeiture of lands, and levied a fine of one thousand pounds. To secure exoneration and a discharge of the heavy sum the anxious inhabitants of Blue Hill proceeded to set forth the difficulties which had rendered impossible the complete fulfilment of their promises.

They have been, they state, under great expense in "trying to Procure His Majesty's Approbation," which the General Court demanded. Moreover, they were under great "Discomfiture, even Suffering" during the years of the War when their man power was depleted for the Continental Army and when the settlement, because of the British holding of the neighbouring lands on Penobscot Bay, was cut off from the protection of Massachusetts. They further call the attention of the "Honourables of the General Court" to the fact that they have not entirely neglected the fulfilment of the original terms since "except in the time of the late War" they have hired "a Preacher every Summer for Seventeen Years and a Scholemaster every Winter." Perhaps, indeed, they felt with some justice that the presence of the one compensated for the absence of the other! At all events their explanation was accepted, and they continued to survive, even to flourish, yet another ten years under "Four Months annually of the Gospel so that our children may not grow up like the Heathen."

In the autumn of 1795, however, they decided "to settle a Minister" and immediately made overtures to one, Jonathan Fisher of Braintree, Massachusetts, who had already preached among them during the preceding summer. Their proposals to this ardent man of God, whose residence for fifty-one years in Blue Hill was to prove so telling in its influence upon several generations, are not without interest:

October 16, 1795.

Voted, at a special Town-Meeting called for the purpose, that the Church in this town be desired to appoint a Committee at their meeting on Tuesday next to wait upon Mr. Jonathan Fisher and make him the following Proposals to settle in this town, viz:—

That the town will allow him one hundred and twenty pounds cash with no barn, or sixty pounds cash and build him a barn forty by thirty feet as a settlement, and that they will also allow him Sixty pounds yearly as a Salary and fall and Clear for him five acres of land yearly on the Minister's lot for ten years; and that after the expiration of the said ten years they will allow him Eighty pounds yearly as a Salary during his services to this town as their Minister; and that he may absent himself from the Service of the Church five weeks in each and every year.

Not a little of the shrewdness, practicality, and candour of the Reverend Mr. Fisher, then aged twenty-seven years, is evident in his reply. Already on the ground of his future pastorate, he took six days to weigh the matter pro and con until on the twenty-second of October he sent his answer to the town:

To the Inhabitants of the Town of Blue Hill,

Gentlemen:—Having received your proposals for settling in the Ministry among you and having taken a view of the lot of land reserved for the first Minister; the settlement and salary appear to be generous and equal to my expectations, considering the infancy of the country.

In the land I am somewhat disappointed, it being much of it broken, and containing but little timber. Considering this last circumstance, I hope the town will not be offended, nor think it unreasonable, if I request that the proposals stand as follows, viz:—

That the town will allow him two hundred dollars cash and build him a barn forty by thirty feet, of thirteen feet and a large stud, and finish it completely as a settlement, and that they will also allow him two hundred Dollars as Salary yearly, and cut and haul fifteen cords of hard wood, eight feet in length, and fall and clear five acres of land on the Minister's lot yearly for ten years.

That after the expiration of the said ten years, they will allow him two hundred and fifty Dollars as Salary, and cut and haul thirty cords of hard wood, eight feet in length yearly, during his services to this town as their Minister; that a full payment of the Salary for each and every year be made before the commencement of the year following; that he may absent himself from the services of the Church five weeks in each and every year, and that in the case of time of sickness, he shall not be obliged to make it good; except the time exceeds four weeks yearly.

If these proposals be agreeable to the town, they will be cheerfully accepted on my part, provided I can find my way clear to settle in this town on any conditions.

I request your prayer to God for me, that he would direct and assist me. I can give you encouragement of my accepting your invitation, but request the liberty of deferring a

positive answer until my arrival at the westward (meaning
Boston). Wishing grace, mercy, and peace to attend you,

I am, Gentlemen,

Your Servant in Christ,

JONATHAN FISHER.

Young Mr. Fisher did not enter upon his pastoral
duties until nine months had passed. Those he spent
at Harvard College, from which he had been graduated in 1792, completing his course in Theological
Studies. In June of 1796 he returned to Blue Hill
where his prescribed barn had already been erected
and began at once both his ministerial duties and the
designing and building of his own home.

(2)

No sketch of the religious environment which I
knew as a child can be complete or even accurate
without some presentation of the Reverend Jonathan
Fisher. His was a personality, manifold, trenchant,
permanent. Although he died forty years before I
was born, his influence still remained among us, half
sinister, half auspicious, always engrossing and relentless. It can hardly be given to many to stamp a
community so indelibly as he stamped that of his
adoption. Nor was that impress left only about the
confines of Blue Hill Bay. He was known in Bangor
where he was a trustee of the Theological Seminary;
in Brunswick where he left his mark on Bowdoin
College; in Boston and in his college in Cambridge.
In the second volume of Sprague's *Annals of the*

American Pulpit, a volume, like the first, given to the biographies of distinguished Congregational clergymen of the Trinitarian persuasion, his life and works hold honoured place.[1] And if today, eighty years and more since his death, the authority of his stern Calvinism has ceased, his name at least provokes delighted interest in more communities than one and in other states than the State of Maine.

His genius was, indeed, a multifarious one, mechanical, financial, intellectual, social, spiritual. His energy, as well it must be, was exhaustless. Once arrived in Blue Hill with his young wife, whom he had married six years earlier, he began the erection of a substantial and beautiful home. The design was his own, even to the minutest details; much of the actual building he did himself. During an evening walk he discovered yellow ochre on a portion of the land allotted to him as settlement and was freed from any further anxiety on the score of paint. Practically every piece of furniture he made with his own hands. He constructed a clock which ran for fifty years without repair and with no attention save winding. The study table, upon which he wrote his sermons and the hundreds of "admonitions" which he sent upon occasion here and there about his parish, could be quickly converted into a carpenter's bench with tools ready for use. He built the first windmill

---

[1] Sprague, William B., *Annals of the American Pulpit, or Commemorative Notices of Distinguished Clergymen of Various Denominations, from the Early Settlement of the Country to the Close of the Year 1855.* New York and London, 1857. Vol. II, pp. 344 ff.

in town and, to be served by it, a machine for sawing wood. He made another machine to remove large stones from his fields and yet another to split straw for the fashioning of hats. Engaged for years in the compilation of a Hebrew lexicon, he fashioned his own type in tiny blocks of wood and thereupon printed his own pages. He was, of course, a farmer, raising practically all the food which his family of nine children consumed. He was also the surveyor for the community, utilizing his knowledge of mathematics to accomplish the work made possible by the surveying instruments which he invented. He found leisure to adorn the walls of his dwelling with pictures, to paint a portrait of himself as he sat before a mirror, and to paint also a picture of Harvard College as it was in his days as a student.

Like Goldsmith's parson he found himself "passing rich on forty pounds a year." His abilities as a financier had been early manifested. During his freshman year at Harvard he had constructed birdcages which he turned to pecuniary account. His full expenses during five of the seven years spent at Cambridge, including clothing and books, amounted to six hundred and five dollars. He gave liberally to the early charities of his pastorate and managed at the same time to send several of his daughters to boarding-school and his two sons who grew to manhood to Bowdoin and to Princeton. Finding the purchase of paper for his sermons a large and unnecessary outlay, he devised a system of shorthand which enabled him to write "any ordinary morning's discourse" on one-eighth of a sheet of foolscap. By this economy he saved, according to his meticulous expense account, about seventy dollars in the course of thirty years. His thrift extended to his clothing, for his boast was that he never owned an overcoat and, until his latest years, never wore underwear of any sort.

His intellectual pursuits were never allowed to suffer from the abundance of his manual labours. At college he had shown decided ability in philological studies, and he continued therein, in spite of the meagre advantages of his frontier life. His family devotions were conducted, one day in Hebrew, the next in Greek; occasionally he read from a Latin and from a French version of the Scriptures. His Hebrew lexicon, still in manuscript, remains the great achievement of his life. In his later years he began the study of Arabic. He read his Sunday texts, first in English and then, as the case might be, in Hebrew or in Greek, so that the ears of his congregation "might be whetted by a desire for a more liberal education." He published a little volume entitled *Scripture Animals* and designed for children. At the beginning of each chapter was a picture of the bird, beast, reptile, or insect which he was treating and under the picture in English, Hebrew, Greek, Latin, and French was the name of the creature. He left a volume of poetry in manuscript for each of his surviving children.

Only his contemporary, Wordsworth, could have excelled him in walking. He could not afford to keep

a horse; therefore, most of his travels in pastoral
work and in attendance upon councils and conferences
were on foot. A trustee of the Bangor Theological
Seminary, he apparently thought nothing of walking
the thirty-five miles to Bangor to attend board meetings and ordinations. Once, being informed that a
learned professor of Greek was lecturing at Harvard,
he walked along the coast roads to Cambridge during
a vacation period from preaching to hear his dis-
courses. Ministers being few and far between, he was
often called upon to conduct funerals and to visit the
sick and dying at no small distances and in all those
weathers which only the coast of Maine can produce
and retain. He visited once a year every family in
his far-flung parish for the purpose of catechizing the
children; and he kept a scrupulous record of all
births, deaths, and marriages. Only those who have
traversed frozen, rutty country roads before the advent of state highways can understand fully all that
such journeyings imply!

His social ministrations became early inseparable
from his spiritual; he made himself, in fact, alike the
arbiter of spiritual destinies and the referee of all
social upheavals. His two sermons on Sunday (for
the members of his congregation in accordance with
the custom of the day ate their lunch in the church
or churchyard) seem, in comparison, the least of his
duties. From his papers we gather that upon his arrival he found his parishioners "sadly tending toward Arminianism" and that he drew up a coherent

statement of belief consistent with his own Calvinism, which statement he induced, perhaps better *coerced*, them to sign. One smiles at that lofty word, Arminianism, suspecting that its sonorous dignity concealed only a laxity in faith and good works to which poor human nature is forever heir!

CHAPTER II

THE FRUITFUL CORRESPONDENCE OF
THE REVEREND MR. FISHER

WE cannot be sufficiently grateful to this redoubtable servant of God for the innumerable and exhaustive records which he left, neatly filed and labelled, behind him. Many of these are copies of letters which he wrote to one and another of his erring flock. Through them we are able to glean not only minute details of the life of his parish but also a memorable portrait of himself as the wielder of a big and influential club. No scandal was too small for his interference; no dispute was too insignificant for his intrepid peace-making.

A certain Eben Carleton in the year 1821 was so careless of his position as a professor of religion as to "lay a small bet" on the relative speed of two horses. His pastor sends him an admonition which he heeds to the extent that he rises in meeting the following Sunday to read before his neighbours an acknowledgment and a confession, obviously penned by the hand of Mr. Fisher:

I confess that at a trial of the speed of some horses, held on a Saturday in September, I was so forgetful of my position as a professor of religion as to lay a small bet on one of them. I now clearly see that this act was unbecoming to a Christian and a source of temptation and sin to those around me. I humbly confess my sin, and I ask forgiveness of God and of this church which I have thus offended.

Mr. Israel Wood, who in a fit of temper has had the temerity to call the shepherd of his soul a liar, also rises in church to make amends and to ask forgiveness. Sisters Ellis and Treworgy, ladies who apparently possessed clashing temperaments, are bidden to settle their difficulties straightway lest they become stumbling-blocks to their friends and a dishonour to the name and to the cause of religion. Mrs. Sukey Clay, evidently a member of the local young *intelligentsia,* is informed by letter on November 15th, 1829, that because she has long neglected with insufficient excuse to commune with the church she is "cast out from the visible kingdom of God." "But you have an immortal soul at stake," writes her pastor. "If you be at last excluded from the Kingdom of Glory, your soul may be lost forever. You must be shut up forever in the kingdom of darkness." Such threats were apparently too much for Sukey Clay. Before Christmas she "appeared humbly before the congregation," confessed her sin, and sued equally humbly for reinstatement in a penitential document composed for her by her pastor. In those days, were piety lacking, one might have been lured to church simply on the safe chance of dramatic potentialities!

Entertaining perusal of Mr. Fisher's correspondence proves him a master of the persuasive style.

The letter which follows and which is one of his best was written to a certain Mrs. Roxana Ray on the 3rd of May, 1817:

MADAM:

It is painful to me to have occasion to address you upon the subject which now calls forth my pen. If a sense of duty did not constrain me, I should omit the unwelcome task. But we are bound by covenant to give one another friendly warning, admonition, and reproof. For some time before and some time after you made a profession of religion, I did hope that you had experienced a saving change; from all I could learn, it appeared that you kept your temper, uncomfortable as it naturally is, under a good measure of subjection. I expected it would be a trouble to you, warned you of the danger, and exhorted you to watch against it with all diligence. I did not expect you would again allow yourself in such a long continued and excessive indulgence of angry passions as I am constrained to believe you have. When first called to converse with you on the subject, I thought it expedient to use great mildness, hoping that your heart might relent and that you would be brought to see and to feel the evil of your ways. I did hope that after a little reflection, you would be humbled to the very dust and come again to the entertainment of a meek and amiable disposition. I am sorry that I have been disappointed. I now very much doubt whether you know what it is to be the subject of regeneration. The apostle teaches, "If any one have not the spirit of Christ, he is none of his." Christ says, "Learn of me, for I am meek and lowly in heart."

Where is your exhibition of the spirit of Christ? Where is that self-denial which the gospel requires? Where is that reverence, love, and submission to your husband, which the Word of God inculcates? Read Ephesians 5 from the middle to the end and I Peter, 3 to verse 7, and meditate upon these places: compare then your own temper and spirit with what is there required. What pleasure can it give you to be an affliction to your husband? What satisfaction to be a vexation to the rest of your family? Should you be the means of their eternal condemnation, are you prepared to answer for it in the awful day of judgment? Do you entertain no friendship, no regard for the honor of religion? Are you willing to crucify the Son of God afresh, to put Him to an open shame?

Perhaps you may wish to be separated from your husband; in such case no doubt he would have the prudence to prevent you from involving him in debt; and he has an undoubted right to retain his children with him. How would it appear, should you withdraw from your bosom friend, move away, and live by yourself? I am satisfied that in such case serious people would loathe the very sight of you. Say what you will of your husband's being deceitful, I have no idea but that, if you were to a tolerable measure a kind and faithful wife to him, you would find him a tender, indulgent husband. But if you will persist in endeavoring to usurp authority over him, he will be perfectly justifiable in resisting such an unwarrantable claim. You must not think that you can go voluntarily into a state of separation from your husband consistently with the profession of Christianity, nor continue so consistently with being a Christian; in such case you must certainly be excluded from the church of Christ on earth, and, without repentance, must be excluded from the kingdom of Heaven. Even as it is, your conduct has been so unchristianlike, so long under the control of sinful passion, and so notorious has this been to the world, that you must not expect to be tolerated long in the fellowship of the church in this place, without a serious, public acknowledgment of your fault and a manifestation of a change of life for the better.

You may say I use sharpness. I answer, I feel it now to

be necessary. As the apostle says to the Galatians, I am constrained to change my voice, for I stand in doubt of you. I contemplate you as on the very verge of ruin. Sharp measures I believe to be necessary for your recovery. Gentle measures have not succeeded. If sharp measures fail, I think you will be lost. I solemnly protest unto you, that if you will be contentious and will not obey the truth, indignation and wrath, tribulation and anguish will soon overtake you and press upon you forever! The cup which you have filled for others, God will fill for you double. He will put it into the hands of those fallen spirits, who will delight to rule over you with rigor. They will vex you in every way, and you will cry, yea, *howl*, but you will find no relief, no, none forever!

Dear soul, what is the reason, the ground of the indulgence of these angry passions? It is *self-will*; it is a propensity in us all by nature to wish to be supreme. But self-will, in whatever way it may operate, must be brought into subjection; it must submit, it must be crucified; it must be destroyed or it will destroy us. There is no other alternative. How awful was the resolve of the prince of devils as expressed by Milton: "Better to reign in Hell than to serve in Heaven"!

Madam, you must turn about, you must lead a new life, you must become a comfort to your husband, a blessing to your children, a joy to your neighbors, or by and by you will be consigned to that world of darkness where you will not have the malicious consolation of reigning but must serve with rigor in a state of most abject slavery. I do not wish you to be driven to desperation; but I wish you might feel the awful impropriety of your conduct in such sense as you never yet have felt it, and reform, not with a merely hypocritical and momentary reformation, but with a reformation pleasant as the returning spring and lasting as eternity.

Should you be led through the mercy of God to the exercise of true repentance, to that humility which is deep and sincere, and signify to the church in a proper manner a desire to wipe away the reproach you have cast upon religion, by an explicit, public profession of penitency, you will have opportunity to do it, and I trust may be freely restored to our fellowship. Otherwise, the withered branch must be cut off. If then the just judgment of God confirm the sentence of the church and you be cut off at length by the hand of Divine Justice, what will be your state hereafter? You must dwell with everlasting burnings. And what is it to dwell with everlasting burnings? You don't conceive what it is! You don't realize it. Should you be destroyed, both soul and body in Hell, you will spend an awful eternity weeping and gnashing your teeth and vehemently cursing your past folly. May grace prevent it! Such is the prayer of

Your friend and Pastor,

JONATHAN FISHER.

Like Sukey Clay, Mrs. Ray found it wholesome and expedient for her comfort both in Blue Hill and in the next world to repent. One can imagine the suppressed excitement of a full meeting-house on the June morning when she rose and read her confession, which betrays its author by its style:

I, the subscriber, desire to give glory to God in a humble and penitent confession of those sins, by means of which I have dishonored the name of God and wounded the cause of religion.

Particularly I confess that during the past winter I so far lost the fear of God from before my eyes, and the sense of my obligations to the divine Savior, that I repeatedly gave way to a frame of sinful anger, and to that indulgence of

Bluehill June 5. 1817.

I, the Subscriber, desire to give glory to God in a humble and penitent confession of those sins, by means of which I have dishonored the name of God, and wounded the cause of religion.

Particularly I confess that during the past winter I so far lost the fear of God from before my eyes, and the sense of my obligations to the divine Savior, that I repeatedly gave way to a frame of sinful anger, and to that indulgence of an unholy, unpleasant temper, which for a time greatly interrupted the peace of my family, and rendered me a grief to the children of God around me. I trust that thro' the mercy of God I have been humbled for this conduct, and ask the forgiveness of God, of this Church, and of all I have offended, and pray for grace to walk in time to come in suitable mildness, meekness, & gentleness, to the honor of the religion I have professed.

Roxana   her +   Ray

mark

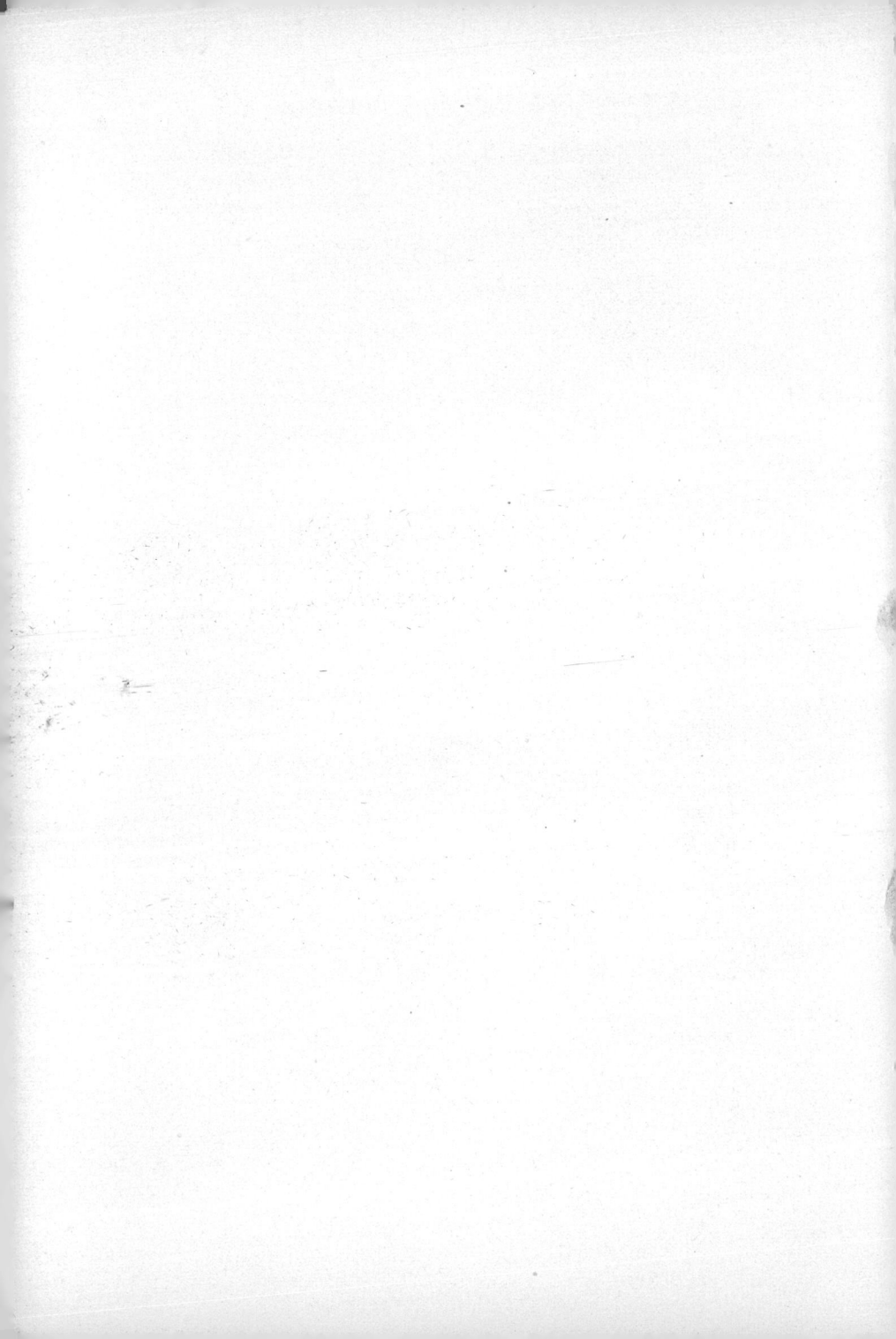

an unholy, unpleasant temper, which for a time greatly interrupted the peace of my family, and rendered me a grief to the children of God about me. I trust that through the mercy of God I have been humbled for this conduct, and ask the forgiveness of God, of this Church, and of all I have offended; and pray for grace to walk in time to come in suitable mildness, meekness, and gentleness, to the honor of the religion I have professed.

ROXANA RAY.

The Reverend Mr. Fisher had not infrequent cause to warn certain of his flock against the ills of intemperance. Not that he himself eschewed a seemly use of intoxicating liquors. Far from it! Among his papers I find a recipe for "An Excellent Cherry Rum," which he apparently concocted from the wealth of wild cherry trees still growing in great profusion along his pasture fence. I find, too, a letter from a daring parishioner charging the minister with wilful waste in that he turned upon his manure-pile from a demijohn at least two quarts of that selfsame rum, "which might have been of health and solace to the ailing among us." When the new church building was completed and dedicated shortly after his arrival in the town (a building modelled on the Old South Church of Boston) he, in accordance with a custom common throughout the seventeenth and eighteenth centuries in Massachusetts, prescribed "a barrel of rum with molasses for sweetening sufficient for raising the meeting-house." But that he believed in moderation of consumption is evinced in the following letter to an immoderate drinker of his parish, one Mr. Freeman Hardin:

January 28th, 1824.

DEAR SIR:

At a meeting of the Brethren of the Church at the meeting-house last Friday evening it was voted that you be suspended for the present from the communion of the Church and that your Pastor give you an admonition.

In compliance with this vote, Dear Sir, and with feelings of no small interest for the honour of the Christian profession and for the everlasting well-being of your immortal soul, I would improve this occasion to warn and admonish you to renounce with deep solicitude every degree of the indulgence of intemperance. Though you may be in the habit of refraining from ardent spirits, you may err by wine; there are other kinds of strong drink besides that which is obtained by distillation. Wines, in ancient times, were almost the only kinds of intoxicating liquors in use. Against them the Scriptures often caution us: Look not thou upon the wine when it is red, when it giveth its color in the cup, when it moveth itself aright. At the last it biteth like a serpent and stingeth like an adder. Proverbs 23: 31, 32.

For the honor of the cause of religion I charge you, Dear Sir, to deny yourself entirely of all intoxicating drink. If there be not in you the firmness to deny yourself, after the evils you have seen resulting from it in your case already, you have very serious reason to fear that you are a stranger to the new birth, that the flesh is not yet nailed to the cross, and that your immortal soul is in danger of being forever lost. O what will you then find to quench your raging thirst, where not a drop of water is allowed to cool a burning tongue? I pray you, don't indulge the natural propensity of man, when reproved, to endeavor to extenuate his faults by appealing to the example of other transgressors. So to do is a dark sign that we are not unfeignedly penitent.

For grace to control your erring will, look daily, sincerely and humbly in secret prayer to God in the name of the Lord Jesus Christ.

From your friend and Pastor,

JONATHAN FISHER.

During the full period of the Reverend Mr. Fisher's ministry the sentence of excommunication was consistently employed as the most extreme measure of discipline. That it was usually successful is proved by the number of public confessions, written in Mr. Fisher's hand and without doubt composed by him, which are filed together with the stern documents of dismissal. One surmises that in so small a community the social embarrassment resulting from being thus singled out from one's fellows was quite as potent a factor as spiritual regeneration in bringing to terms an erring brother or sister! There follows such a sentence of excommunication pronounced against Mr. Joseph Treworgy and dated November 15, 1829:

Sentence of Excommunication against Mr. Joseph Treworgy

In conformity to the instructions of the Holy Scriptures, and in compliance with the vote of the Church in this place, of October 15th, it has become the painful duty of the Pastor of this Church this day to denounce sentence of excommunication against our late Mr. Joseph Treworgy.

Mr. Treworgy, having on the 11th of June last been called before the Church on account of reports unfavorable to his Christian character; and on the 2nd of July it having been proved that in a dispute in the presence of a number of persons he was sinfully angry and exposed himself in a manner much unbecoming a Christian professor and wounding to the cause of Christ, and having been required to offer a confession in public to this amount, and having been labored with several times to lead him to repentance, and having now more than eighteen weeks refused to hear the Church and offer such confession; and the Church also having voted that sentence of exclusion from its fellowship should this day be declared:

In presence of this assembly and before that God who witnesses all our transactions, I now declare Joseph Treworgy to be excluded from this Church, that he is to be to us as a heathen man and a publican; out of the visible kingdom of God, no longer a Christian brother in fellowship with us; no longer entitled to the privilege of Church membership till such time as through repentance and becoming confession he shall be restored.

In the meantime we are bound to refrain from that familiar social intercourse with him which is proper to be maintained with Christian brethren and sisters in the Church.

But while it is our duty to maintain towards him this reservedness, it is also our duty to pray for him and occasionally to admonish him that if it may be, God will give him repentance.

And now, O that he might suitably feel his situation, aggravated by a long refusal to comply with a reasonable requirement and that he might humble himself before God and return to duty!

And may we all, who yet think we stand, take heed lest we fall. May we beware that we do not offend and bring evil upon our souls, and especially may we be concerned that we bring not dishonor upon that name which is above every name, even the name of Christ.

AMEN.

That Mr. Fisher recruited his congregation slowly and with the utmost vigilance is shown by several documents descriptive of the "works of divine grace" experienced by those asking admittance. These explicit proofs of the favour of God were still held by Mr. Fisher, as they were held by the early church in Boston and its vicinity, to be absolutely necessary before a candidate was received into fellowship with God's elect. Thus one, Japheth Littlefield, in June, 1821 failed to convince the assembled church that he had actually received unmistakable marks of divine favour and was invited thereupon to wait until he could offer more conclusive evidence.

"Upon hearing his account of the grace of God towards him," wrote the pastor in his description of the conclave, "I put to him several stout questions to which his answers were not satisfactory to me or to the Brethren. Were his corporeal frame touched as he alleges by divine healing of many ills, why has there not ensued a more vigorous spiritual health?"

Doubtless Mr. Littlefield left the meeting-house on that occasion in some perturbation if not *vexation* of spirit!

The spiritual as well as the social requirements of this early pastor waned with the years. Perhaps the positive proofs of divine revelation waned also. Nevertheless, nearly ninety years later, when I myself at twenty sought admittance to the same body, I also was required, embarrassed and alone on a June evening, to meet a vigilant array of deacons and members in order that I might justify my decision and desire if not by indisputable proofs of divine grace, at least by indisputable evidence of a humble and a contrite spirit!

CHAPTER III

AN EARLY ENCOUNTER WITH THE
HOLY GHOST

LONG before I had reached the age either of assimilation or of reason, I came into contact with the Third Person of the Trinity in a way which can only be termed an encounter. Every detail of the occasion is today as clear in my mind as is the occurrence of a morning when it is reviewed at evening: the time, the scene, the agent, the cruelly tangible and material means of my introduction.

The meeting took place in the fall of 1893 when I was approaching my sixth birthday; the scene was the home of a neighbour; the agent, our neighbour herself, an elderly, stately woman known to us as Great-Aunt Anna Hinckley. My years were thin indeed in comparison with the long accumulated ones which she had experienced as the wife and the widow of Captain Thomas Hinckley, an eminent sea-captain and merchant of Blue Hill. Like my grandmother, she had spent many of her earliest years at sea; but unlike my grandmother she had gained therefrom not so much a quickening sense of life and of the variegated pattern of the world as a deadening knowledge of the wickedness in high and in low places and a sense of her duty as a pillar and ground of the truth. As she prepared herself daily in the stern orthodoxy of her fathers for death and the Judgment Seat, so she strove to fit all children and young people for a thoroughly uncomfortable and anxious existence. The rather flighty ways of my grandmother, several years her junior, were a source of constant and scrupulous concern to her.

A prey to rheumatism and its attendant ills, she was confined during her later years to her chair in an upper room of the great white house above our own. She was a very large, beautifully-complexioned woman with grey, piercing eyes below smoothly parted hair, held in place on the top of her head by a high tortoise shell comb. In the morning she wore a white cap and a grey percale dress; in the afternoon, no cap, a basque of black silk or satin, and a long, full skirt covered inevitably by a spotless white apron. She read her Bible constantly, culling from it the stern sobriety and zeal which made her presence awful. She it was who first acquainted me with the Holy Ghost.

I had gone to play one early November afternoon with her grandchildren, Thomas and Eldusta Hinckley. It was Saturday, and there was no one else in the great, rambling house but ourselves and her. An early snow storm made playing out-of-doors for children as young as we inadvisable, and we looked about for means of amusement within. Suggestion offering itself from the recent Hallowe'en parties which the older boys and girls had enjoyed, we decided to play at being ghosts; and we were summarily assisted by the laden clothes-baskets awaiting Monday in the cold buttery. Dragging sheets and table-cloths into the kitchen, we arrayed ourselves in white and proceeded to ape our elders by shrieks and moans as we ran hither and yon through the house.

Since the initial idea of the game had originated with me, I was quick to seize upon any mark of pre-eminence to distinguish myself from Thomas and Eldusta. Somewhere in the back of my small mind, born from Bible readings, from the Sunday rendering of the Doxology, from Golden Texts, or perchance from stray words of many a sermon, there existed a name and a perception of such distinction.

"You cannot be the *Holy* Ghost," I cried to Thomas and Eldusta. "I shall be him and tell *you* what to do."

How dearly I paid for such presumption, for such irresponsible, unconscious blasphemy! For as we ran through the rooms upstairs and down under my guidance and inspiration, the sound of Great-Aunt Anna's bell summoned us to her chair. I can see us now as we trailed into her presence, half-frightened, half-triumphant over our grown-up ways; I can see the puzzled look in her eyes as she raised them from the black Bible on her full white lap, hear her deep questioning voice.

"What are you children playing in those sheets, Thomas?"

"Ghost!" yelled Thomas. He was a fat, round-faced little boy, and, overwrought with excitement, he did not temper his reply.

"A very singular game," said Great-Aunt Anna, "and a noisy one."

I felt even at six that some explanation was due, and I summoned my courage and my voice. I felt, too, even though the situation seemed portentous, no small degree of pride in the distinction I had conferred upon myself.

"They are only ghosts," I explained carefully. "But I—I am the *Holy* Ghost!"

Even though by reason of strength my years become three score and ten, I shall never forget one detail of what followed. The sinister atmosphere of that square, white-panelled room can still smother me. I can still breathe that silence, ever growing deeper and thicker, can hear the ticking of the clock on the mantel-piece, and the faint, intermittent clicking of the sleet as it was blown against the window-pane. I knew then for the first time in my life what it was to await the inevitable.

Great-Aunt Anna took time to choose her words. It is but fair to her terrifying memory to say that she doubtless felt her duty summoning her to slow and careful action. Her genuine distress was betokened by a pink spot in either cheek which deepened to red while we waited by her chair. When she spoke at last, she addressed only me, relieved perhaps that the children of her own flesh were relatively guiltless, were at worst more sinned against than sinning.

"You have said a very wicked thing, my child. When you are older, you will know *how* wicked. God has struck people in this Book dead for less than for what you have said. Go home, now, *very slowly*, and ask Him to forgive you."

Her words lay like weights inside my poor little body. They dragged at my feet as I stumbled down the long, curving stairs, followed by Thomas and Eldusta; they made my fingers unwieldy and awkward as I tried to divest myself in the kitchen of my ghostly apparel. Thomas brought my coat in silence and Eldusta my hood. It was grey, I remember, with a piquant blue bow on the forehead and blue ribbons beneath the chin. I had worn it that day for the first time, but my pride in it was now as dead as I might be at any moment. Considering my sin and their own innocence, Thomas and Eldusta showed great mercy and lovingkindness to me, tying my hood and holding out my blue mittens for my cold little hands and fingers. In utter silence I was arrayed, and in silence as complete they opened the door for me to go home down the long, snow-covered hill.

Perhaps more vividly than any other detail, I remember the care with which I lifted my poor little feet, up and down, down and up, through the wet, heavy snow. I had interpreted Great-Aunt Anna's threatening command to mean that my life might depend upon the nature of my progress,—that if I moved as slowly as possible, God might spare me the terrible penalty of this strange sin which all unwittingly I had committed. Down and up, up and down, I moved my feet, slowly, deliberately, precisely. No care, I determined, should be wanting on my part. If to move slowly was to save me from His anger, slowly I would move.

I reached our driveway at last. How interminably it stretched beneath the black, swaying elms! At last I reached our warm fragrant kitchen with the lively red geraniums in the window, the brown bread steaming in the kettle on the stove, the beans giving generous signs of their sizzling in the oven. My mother was away on her Saturday marketing; my father was in his office. If any children were about, I do not recall them. Sarah, red-cheeked and stolid, helped me off with my coat, hood and leggings, scolding meanwhile at my lack of assistance. Little she knew of the revengeful presence of God at my elbow!

But Great-Aunt Anna's command was only partially fulfilled. Prayer must follow, alone and in secret. It was one thing to die, if die I must, amid the odour of beans and brown bread, in the presence of Sarah, who with her square shoulders, her big, knobby hands, might conceivably be a match for any average angel of the Lord; it was quite another to be struck dead alone in my icy room beside my patchwork quilt. Nevertheless, "what must be shall be" was as certain a text to me in that hour as to Juliet under no worse burden, in no more dire straits. My things hung in the entry on the peg allotted to me, I went, still slowly, up the stairs to my room and knelt in the cold beside my bed. I remember that I could not summon sufficient courage to bow my head upon my arms. If God or His angel, or this strange connection of His, the Holy Ghost, Whose name I had taken in vain, were to strike me dead, I wanted to be aware of the approaching blow. Thus I was obedient to the apostle's injunction, for, ignorant of the hour when the Lord might come, I was determined to watch as well as to pray!

I did not tell my parents what had befallen me. Those were days when punishments were meted out for wrongdoing of any kind, and I had every reason to believe myself in a punishable state. My mother, seeing my flushed cheeks at supper and noting my lack of appetite, administered aconite pellets from her homeopathic chest and put me early to bed. I lay in the dark, listening to the November wind, sick with terror. From somewhere I had heard that dead people were cold. Conversely, I thought, as I held my freezing feet stiff against the bedclothes, cold people must be about to die. Doubtless the smiting of the Lord was to be of slow duration, had, in fact, already begun! When my older sister crawled in beside me and I heard almost immediately her warm, easy breathing, which betokened an untarnished conscience, I sensed, also for the first time in my life, the bitterness of irony!

It was months before fear ceased to torment me,

fear of God and of the righteous anger of my parents should they learn of my sin. Truly, the way of the transgressor is hard, and harder was the way of the innocent one! A yet more bitter irony was in store for me when long afterward my apprehensive ears heard the minister in the Sunday morning Bible reading refer to the Holy Ghost as the "comforter." I was far too wise to think as did my younger sister that the Lord had sent a bed-quilt to His disciples! But though I could refute her ignorant conception, I could not for all my superior wisdom explain either to her or to myself wherein lay the comfort of His strange messenger, Whose name must never, under any circumstances, be uttered by children at play.

CHAPTER IV

THE LORD'S DAY IN THE NINETIES

(1)

TO all Protestant communities in rural New
England during the nineties (and in the State of
Maine there was almost no distinctly rural community which was not wholly Protestant) Sunday was
unmistakably the Lord's Day. That we were glad
and rejoiced therein cannot be claimed with the same
degree of certainty. Foretaste, perhaps even fore-
boding, of Sunday began with our Saturday dinner,
which was invariable. It consisted of salt fish boiled
in a cloth bag and in a pot well filled with potatoes.
This sustenance, commonly known in New England
as "Cape Cod turkey," was served with a generous
supply of hot pork scraps floating in a bowl of equally
hot grease. Strangers to Maine ways who came to our
table often had to be shown how to shred the fish on
their plates, how to mash their potatoes, how to pour
upon the mixture the pork gravy. Under my mother's cooking the result was not only palatable but
delicious. This meal had originated many years before because it made possible the Sunday dinner without undue labour on that day. In the afternoon the

large remainder was made into fish-balls and set in a cool place to await the morrow.

Another foretaste of Sunday came, in our large family, immediately after dinner was cleared away. By two o'clock the weekly bathing began. Before the turn of the century no house in Blue Hill possessed a bath-room. Ours, the first in town, was installed when I was seventeen, and its exciting installation followed a law-suit of several years' standing in which we became involved because of our inordinate desire for a water supply of our own. There was no town water supply; indeed, there is not to this day; and one paid dearly both financially and emotionally for any rebellion against wells, cisterns, or pasture springs.

The weekly bath, therefore, was fraught with inconvenience and difficulty; nevertheless, in all well-regulated families, the omission of it was inconceivable. Although in warmest weather the sea proved helpful, a salt water bath by tacit consent of all the "best people" was looked upon with suspicion as not fulfilling the requirements either of cleanliness or of moral and religious duty. Custom and time alike had prescribed a washtub by the kitchen stove; and time and custom in the nineties were not lightly set aside.

One by one we scrubbed ourselves or were scrubbed, the odour of the warm soap-suds mingling with the smell of the beans in the oven. One by one we arrayed ourselves or were arrayed in clean underwear and fresh, well-mended stockings. If we finished early, we were encouraged to play at temperate games, to spend an hour at a neighbour's house, or to read quietly in our corners of the library. Riotousness on late Saturday afternoons was frowned upon; it was too much like jocularity after the performance of a sacred rite. On Saturday evenings it was with a sense of corporate decency and order that we gathered around the supper table—a sense which modern plumbing with all its comforts cannot produce.

Sundays in all seasons dawned soberly. Toys of all kinds had been put away in closed drawers or in the corners of the stable. To allow a sled or a cart in the driveway was unthinkable. After a somewhat later breakfast of warmed-over beans and brown bread, we prepared for church and Sunday school, warned of such necessity by the nine o'clock bells which pealed alternately from the two white steeples on opposite hills. In our earlier years my mother, for the sake of family integrity, forsook her Baptist heritage and accompanied her husband, mother-in-law, and children to the Congregational church.

Our family left the house shortly after 10:15 as we must be ascending the church steps by the time the sombre tolling of the last bell began just before the half hour. My father always walked a bit ahead of the rest of us. In all seasonable weather he wore a top hat and a black frock coat, and he carried a gold-headed cane. My mother, often flurried a bit by her morning's undertaking, always had very pink cheeks as she brought up the rear. The appearance of us children varied only with the change from fall and winter to late spring and summer. We each had one best costume and we wore it. My father having a passion for blue serge, which he bought by the bolt, our winter dresses were often fashioned from this material, my mother cleverly disguising one frock from another by bands, braids, pipings, and divergence in pattern. In the summer we wore white or sprigged muslins and wide leghorn hats. The blue serge of my brothers did not change with any season although occasionally it was alleviated by trousers of white duck. We went silently down the country road, skirting a wide field on the right filled with violets, or daisies, or goldenrod, and climbed the hill to the church. At the door we met my grandmother, whose sedate and solitary progress had been accomplished earlier since she liked to confer with her friend, the sexton, over the morning lesson assigned to the minister's Bible class.

Our pew was taxed to its capacity to hold us in the nineties, and as years elapsed we spilled over into another. We had certain rules which we followed in regard to occupation and behaviour during the long morning service. Children up to the age of six were encouraged to sit on crickets throughout the sermon and draw or look at pictures; from six to ten years they might read their Sunday-school books; from ten on they must sit quietly and at least pretend attention. During the hymns, the responsive reading, and the long prayer all of whatever age must listen and participate in so far as each was able. My father not infrequently annoyed my mother after the sermon had gone on for three-quarters of an hour by turning in his corner seat at the outside of our pew to look at the great circular clock which hung below the choir gallery; but if we perchance followed his bad example, we were admonished by a shake of her head or, for that matter, of his own.

Although church provided in the nineties no such dramatic possibilities as it had promised in the days of the Reverend Jonathan Fisher, it was not entirely bereft of excitement. Once my brother Edward, deep in his Sunday-school book, and forgetful of his surroundings, laughed aloud in the midst of the sermon. This act, however, which my father singularly enough allowed to go unreproved, was as nothing compared to the consternation and embarrassment which he caused us all on one memorable day. Seized by a spirit of defiance and of rebellion unknown among us, he had on the morning in question purposely hitched himself in his white duck trousers around on the grass of the lawn until their seat was a sight to behold. Our hearts stood still as my father, issuing from the house, beheld this proof of insurrection. But instead of the swift retribution which we expected, my brother was forced to walk to church and to stand, during the Doxology and the hymns, on the highest cricket, his pants in full view of the congregation. The mortification which we as a family experienced on that devastating occasion can never be minimized or forgotten! Surely one cannot pay singly for his own transgressions!

My grandmother also afforded drama, now amusing to recollect but then embarrassing to undergo. As she grew older and the deafness which crept early upon her became more acute, a certain practice of hers was a source of no little confusion. Since she contributed fifty dollars yearly to the support of the minister, an amount almost unheard of in those days and equalled only by a certain well-to-do parishioner, Mrs. Harriet Morton by name, she made it an unchangeable rule to place no offering at all in the contribution plate. Her generosity and her habit alike being well and favourably known to the entire community, she was upheld by public sentiment. Imagine then her distress when her rival in good works developed suddenly and without fair warning the custom of giving also some coin as the plate was passed. Not to be outdone, my grandmother prepared with reluctance but with commendable spirit to do the same; her refusal, however, to give one jot or tittle more than her neighbour was destined sorely to test the ingenuity and the peace of mind of the grandchild who sat next her.

Mrs. Morton sat across the aisle and one pew ahead of our own. The task of the child next my grandmother was to ascertain the amount of the coin which she drew from her black reticule and placed upon the plate and to communicate its size to my grandmother before the arrival of the deacon who collected the alms on our side of the church. This information was not so difficult to procure as it might have been in view of the fact that our respective pews were at the extreme front; but the conveying of it require no little ingenuity. It was usually given by signs, one finger signifying a nickel, two a dime, the full hand (a gesture very rarely displayed!) a quarter. But as my grandmother grew older and more hard of hearing, the nervousness engendered by this trying situation increased until, forgetting her deafness, she would say in a voice perfectly audible to the entire congregation, though unheard by herself, "How much did Hattie Morton give *this* morning?" I regret to say, moreover, that neither her voice nor her intonation was strictly in keeping with the ideal atmosphere of a Christian edifice.

After all, the most unalloyed, if less exciting, drama occurred every Sunday morning when my father made his contribution. This was a never failing source of pride to us; for as coins were drawn from pockets and from purses, my father invariably procured from one small pocket at the bottom of his waistcoat a new one-dollar bill and laid it upon the plate. The amount and the occasion alike were too momentous to allow comment at any time. We should have liked to know how he obtained always a new note, how he managed to afford such a prodigious offering. But we never asked, only remained secure in the social and financial distinction which his weekly act conferred upon us.

I do not know that the church service itself engendered much religion within us. The sermons were long and abstruse, and, even as I grew older, I do not recall any which meant much to me. But the solemnity of the occasion, the observance together of a custom, the sense of well-being and of well-doing —memories of these I would not be without. Details, too, impressed themselves on my mind and in my imagination to bring later their longer, richer consequences: the black shadows of birds passing and repassing behind the coloured glass of a memorial window; the sunlight lying in bright, precise figures across the pulpit steps; the order and beauty of the white panelled pews with their polished, mahogany railings; the words and the imagery of old hymns. Most of all I remember verses of the Bible as they were read by the singularly beautiful voice of the old pastor whom I knew throughout my childhood. Sometimes the sonorous quality of the words themselves quite apart from their sense stayed long with me:

"Wherefore, seeing we also are encompassed about by so great a cloud of witnesses . . ."

"The former treatise have I made, O Theophilus. . . ."

"Now faith is the substance of things hoped for, the evidence of things not seen."

Once when I was hardly ten I was startled, aroused from my wandering thoughts, by the awful discovery, the stupendous announcement, that some-

one had actually *seen* the Lord. This was the prophet
Isaiah in the year that King Uzziah died; but for the
moment, so convincing was his voice, I felt sure it
was our minister himself—that in his black coat and
white linen necktie he, the Reverend Ebenezer Bean,
had been before that great throne, high and lifted up,
in that train which filled the temple. As he read, I
felt a tingling sensation down my back, the tiny hairs
rising in my excitement. In one of those inexplicable
feats of memory, the words were stamped henceforth
indelibly upon my mind.

"Above it stood the seraphim; each had six wings;
with twain he covered his face, and with twain he
covered his feet; and with twain he did fly.

"And one cried to another saying, 'Holy, Holy,
Holy, is the Lord of hosts. The whole earth is full
of His glory.'"

(2)

After Sunday-school, which followed hard upon
church, we came home either to change our dresses
or to cover them with large aprons and to await the
Sunday dinner. There was no possible surprise engendered by this anticipation, for we knew precisely
what we were to have. Fishballs browned in a spider
formed the dinner proper. They came on the table
garnished with parsley and interspaced with hard-
boiled eggs cut in white and yellow circles. With
them were served raw onions in vinegar and large
plates of beautifully browned and buttered toast, each
plate being covered ceremoniously with a spotless

white napkin. For dessert there were always pre-
serves of some sort and cake. This dinner had been
for many years a custom in the family, since its
preparation was so slight as to make no one miss
church on account of it and since its actual cooking
could be accomplished on Saturday.

Unlike many other children, even as late as the
nineties we were not forbidden to read anything we
liked on Sundays; indeed, we were encouraged to
spend many a Sunday afternoon with our books.
Often, too, during the six months she spent yearly
with us, my grandmother told us sea stories. This
occupation, because of her own dramatic personality,
partook of the nature of a rite rather than of a pastime. It was performed on summer days in the apple
orchard, my grandmother sitting in a low red chair
beneath a black silk parasol. Other children of the
neighbourhood stood about with us, like attendant
acolytes in an entranced circle while her voice rose
and fell, now in tales of shipwreck, now in many-
hued pictures of Cadiz by moonlight, of the
strangely-coloured birds of the South Seas, of fish
flying through green waves touched with sunset.
Quite different and far less appealing was the Junior
Christian Endeavor meeting which in my childhood
was held in the vestry of the church at three o'clock.
This we always attended, reciting Bible verses memorized for the occasion. We were also encouraged to
make "testimonies," not of our religious experience,

for excepting in rare cases of early conversion we were not supposed to have "experienced" religion, but of our childish aspirations toward that state of Grace. Before or after this meeting, depending upon the season, we often went on our family drive. If that entertainment for some reason or other were lacking, we walked, occasionally with reliable friends of our own age. The favourite place of these Sunday rambles was the cemetery. Whether the day had actually engendered within us a kind of pensive melancholy which was satisfied by such a retreat, I do not know. Perhaps the beautiful location of the spot above the bay with the Mount Desert hills tumbling to the southward had quite as much to do with our choice. But that we chose to walk there often I have undeniable proof in that the dead of my native village, after many years' absence, are more familiar to me than are the living!

On rainy or snowy Sundays there was always the Bible game, the answer to every green card of which by the time I was thirteen I knew by heart. There was also the spelling match designed especially for Sabbath enjoyment. My mother occasionally on stormy Sundays made candy for us while my father took an afternoon nap. More frequently she popped corn, allowing us our share in this delightful operation, so that when my father returned to Creasy or the *Iliad* by the library table he might find a yellow bowl of well-salted puffed kernels at his elbow. In the evening as we grew older we might attend the seven o'clock prayer meeting with my grandmother, although this finish to the day was never insisted upon by our parents.

But the one unalterable rule of the household was that we were to do no manner of week-day work other than that absolutely necessary. My mother could not have brought herself to touch her great sewing-basket even to sew on buttons or to mend a sudden rip. Clothes were carefully inspected on Saturday to forestall any such trying emergencies. Indeed, there seemed to exist in those days an especial Nemesis which brooded over the performance of any sort of handiwork on Sunday. Perhaps an incident which occurred when I was twelve and which made a lasting impression upon me will serve as an adequate illustration of this sinister viewpoint.

The measles, rampant in the village, smote at once all of us children, then numbering five. It being winter time, the question of caring for us in rooms decently warm for sickness engaged my anxious mother, who finally decided to move all her patients downstairs and to convert the parlour and the library into a hospital. The nature of the epidemic was severe, and the convalescence correspondingly slow. What to do with five fractious children, all peeling and itching at the same time, constituted a major problem. We could not read, and even although my mother could set aside household cares long enough to read to us, it was not easy to entertain all by means of the same book. We were forbidden to get out of bed because of drafts or to keep our arms sufficiently from under our bed-clothes to cut paper-dolls or to play games. In the midst of these manifold perplexities my father returned on Saturday from some days at holding court in the county seat, bearing with him my mother's salvation in the shape of five knitting-machines and a quantity of yarns in safe and soothing colours.

To all middle-aged readers of these pages such knitting-machines will bring familiar remembrance. They were small circular objects, a little more than an inch in height and an inch and a half in diameter, painted blue, red, or green. A round hole in the centre was surrounded at equal intervals by curved steel uprights like imbedded wire hairpins. Two strands of yarn were wound about these, and the knitting began by means of a hairpin, the lower strand being lifted over the higher to the inside edge of the uprights. In due course of time there formed within the hole and was drawn below it a small circular tubing of yarn, which after much knitting might form horse-reins or a cord for one's mittens. The use of these machines was very popular in my childhood, although in late years I have hunted for them in vain.

When my father entered our well-populated sick rooms on that late Saturday afternoon and displayed his timely gifts, we were jubilant. Here at last was something to do. Propped on pillows and still extremely well covered, we could, with safety, ply our knitting and thus occupy many tedious hours. My mother also was visibly relieved. Busy hands could not scratch, and busy minds would not be so likely to engender the desire to scratch and to merit thereby the necessary reproofs.

But even with pleasure so near at hand anxiety seized us all. With the lamps already lighted, knitting that evening was out of the question. Could knitting-machines be used with safety and decorum on the Lord's Day? Simultaneously, the question sprang to the lips of all of us. My father, often inadvertent in his replies and quick decisions, answered immediately in the affirmative in spite of the obvious hesitation of my mother. Alas! He was forced to eat his words! My mother might, in view of the fortnight she had endured, have been won over to his point of view; in fact, she was visibly yielding when my grandmother appeared upon the scene.

Now my grandmother was, as has been said, an eclectic in religious matters. Her theology, if, indeed, she possessed anything so erudite, neither deterred nor frightened, neither solaced nor confirmed her. But even in her delightful and volatile mind there existed certain deeply-rooted convictions, just as in her soul there burned with a steady glow certain invincible aspirations, fed daily by the inexhaustible fuel of custom, tradition and practice. Knitting on Sunday, even as a prescription against ill-health and peevish dispositions, had never for one moment been condoned within the precincts of her home; and she was morally and emotionally unable to sanction it.

The five knitting-machines stood in a row on the

library mantel all through an interminable Sunday. That much she was willing to allow. Credit should also be given for her generous attempts to amuse us. She read for hours and, after we tired of books, told us innumerable sea stories, rehearsing the familiar ones with expert embroidering and from her abundant and rampant imagination inventing new ones, which doubtless had small basis in literal truth. And on Monday she was ardent in her promotion of our knitting, winding the skeins of yarn into balls for us after she had placed each on the back of an appropriate chair.

It is difficult, indeed, today when tenseness of thought and of action has almost annihilated intensity of conviction, to find in my grandmother's unequivocal stand anything except amusement. In Mr. Samuel Eliot Morison's satisfying book, *Builders of the Bay Colony*, he praises the Puritans not for the nature of their religious beliefs and principles, but for the ruthless fervour with which they held to them. Perhaps, indeed, my zealous, fruitless search for tencent knitting-machines as gifts to my nephews and nieces can be easily explained. Surely in these days of electric trains and aeronautic inventions of every sort most children would scorn so sedative a pleasure as knitting even on their emancipated Sundays. Is not, therefore, the reason for my continued quest only that I may rediscover from my whimsical and humorous contemplation of such a symbol something of the moral force behind my grandmother's ultimatum in the year 1898?

CHAPTER V

THE PAINFUL EMBARRASSMENT OF
SALVATION

WHEN I was twelve, I made a radical and sweeping change in the nature of the wish which the first star on clear evenings always prompted in my breast. Heretofore, I had desired tangible things, a new book, a birthday party, a trip to Augusta with my father. Now I found myself desiring vehemently that I might become a Christian. Not for anything would I have confided this secret longing to any member of my family. I said in my heart that it must be mine alone. In a moment of confidence, however, I divulged it one summer night to my bosom friend only to find that she, too, had of late been framing the identical aspiration.

To those familiar with the religious anxieties and expectations of communities such as ours in the period of which I write, such wishes will not mark my confidante and me as in any sense abnormal children, unless, indeed, our time, circumstances, and environment were abnormal. We were, as a matter of fact, quite true to type. We knew from the experiences of older brothers, sisters, and friends that, once one had reached the teens, the matter of one's salvation

148

loomed near at hand. There was far more in our wishes on the evening star than aspiration toward a state of Grace. In the very word "Grace" itself lay uneasy speculations and no little apprehension. Simple had been our procedure could we have announced our decision and desire to the church and have been received forthwith into the company of God's elect. But such in our day was not the accepted manner of salvation. First of all, we must be converted, must be made conscious of an overwhelming change within ourselves wrought by this very Grace of God—that strange, spiritual force which had been defined by Saint Paul, was constantly extolled by the minister, was seemingly familiar to most of our elders, but which was so incomprehensible to us. If it were long withheld from us, for, like young Titus, we understood early there was no salvation without it, we became objects of suspicious anxiety to those who were responsible for our spiritual well-being; if it were vouchsafed to us, full and free, after the necessary preliminary steps had been taken, we were doomed to suffer embarrassment indescribable through the "rejoicings" of our elders and the curious attention of our families. In either case, we must suffer discomfort; there was no way out. The Protestant youth of the nineties, both unregenerate and reborn, reared under any brand of non-conformity, understood the meaning of soul-searchings! Surely Saint Augustine and John Calvin caused less confusion to those unbaptized infants whom they con-

demned to mitigated torments than they caused to
the adolescents of my day and generation by their
learned and relentless utterances on the prevenient
Grace of God—utterances dutifully interpreted for
us by the Reverend Jonathan Fisher and his succes-
sors.

Conversion in the nineties was not considered, as
it is today, one of those varieties of religious experience interesting alike to the philosopher and to the
psychologist. Instead, in communities like our own
where philosophy was relatively unknown and psychology, even as a term, practically unheard of, it
was regarded as a necessary and fearfully important
occurrence in one's life, usually undergone in adolescence but sometimes sadly, yea, *dangerously*, deferred until maturer years. The conversion of the
young in their parishes was the deepest concern of
both our ministers; and machinery was each year set
in operation by means of which it might be facilitated.
This machinery consisted always of the January
Week of Prayer and not infrequently also of revival
meetings, held whenever the fields seemed especially
ripe for harvest. The ministers were assisted by the
most ardent souls in their respective congregations,
usually women, who were for the most part honestly
and zealously eager to do the Lord's work as they
saw it. Occasionally, too, the services of a travelling
evangelist were secured, since it was generally con-
ceded that the threats and the pleadings of a stranger
were often more productive of results.

This first week in January was, throughout my young adolescence, the most dramatic period of the year. It was a period fraught with emotion and embarrassment, tense with excitement. Studies and lessons which engaged our attention at all other times were practically set aside during those seven days,—sacrificed, as it were, to the well-being of our immortal souls. Life at school was strained and unnatural. Serious consultations were held with one's best friends before the sessions opened; during recesses one not infrequently listened to the tearful revelations of a close associate who had, the evening before, been touched by the Spirit, or to the equally tearful fears of another who could not quite bring herself to "take the first step." Romantic preferences during this week were always more in evidence. Notes of affection and of extreme concern were passed surreptiously from seat to seat; and many a youth doubtless confused his growing love for the anxious writer with his need and desire for spiritual rebirth. Those who had signified by various participations in the meeting of the preceding night that they had come to a realization of their sins and were ready to lead a new life were subjected the next morning to the curious scrutiny of all their companions. Truly, it took a stout heart to traverse that school-room to one's own uncomfortable seat! Even the assurance of complete regeneration could not banish cruel self-consciousness and embarrassment.

It is impossible to characterize adequately those

January meetings, and quite as impossible to forget a detail of them. They began at seven o'clock so as to allow ample time for the inevitable "after-meeting" of those who were at last ready for the reception of God's Grace. Their procedure was simple and in no sense undignified save when a visiting evangelist had been badly chosen. The two pastors who watched over the spiritual destinies of the town during my childhood and young girlhood were not sensationalists, with all their zeal. Hymns were sung by the congregation, fervent prayers were said by the officiating minister or ministers. These invocations were to many of us the barometer of the evening. Sometimes they were so impassioned, of such an electrical quality, that it seemed to us who listened anxiously as though God would be *forced* to respond,—and with an abundant measure of that mysterious possession or part of Himself, that Grace which was so indispensable. The prayer, indeed, together with the atmosphere which it did or did not produce, marked the tone and tenor, in a word the "success," of the meeting. It was followed by a discourse, which often took upon itself the nature of the prayer in its manner and which, in its matter, varied little. The one fact which was stressed was the inevitability of salvation, since life apart from God was so set about by dangers and disasters, culminating in death, which might be sudden with no time for preparation, and since life with Him was so full of rejoicing. Defer the day and hour though we might, shut ourselves if we would yet another year in our sinfulness, eventually we *must* be brought to our knees at His mercy-seat to receive the joy, gladness, and complete freedom of conscience which flowed therefrom in ever-increasing streams. To our over-wrought, apprehensive minds this rejoicing, this joy and gladness, this freedom from anxiety, though alluring in the extreme, was not particularly evident in the saved about us, at least on such occasions as these.

The high point of the evening, upon which the climax of the after-meeting depended, was reached when the invitation was finally given. Response was in three degrees, resembling the positive, comparative and superlative of our grammars. Those who, conscious of their sins and desirous of leading a better life, signified the same by rising, denoted the first degree. If they were urged within themselves to the point of walking forward, they were adjudged full penitents, candidates for the after-meeting. If they stayed for the after-meeting, they were held to be saved unless, indeed, Grace was withheld from them.

It is difficult, indeed, to recall those after-meetings without resentment, tempered though it has come to be by humour. One great source of embarrassment lay in the fact that penitents were placed in the awkward situation of witnessing a curious anomaly. Neighbours whose reserve had always been heretofore imperturbable, cast restraint to the winds, spoke personally to us about the most delicate matters, pleaded with us, wept, prayed. The awkwardness increased when we were bidden to fall upon our knees, to cast everything upon the mercy of God. We saw the hysterical hearts of friends and playmates unmasked and added our own emotion to the general spiritual turmoil. Embarrassment increased as after more prayers, often centred specifically upon one or another of us, the ministers and their assistants began to make inquiry as to the renewal of our souls. Were we conscious of quickening life? Had God, indeed, spoken to us? Were we new creatures by His Grace? Were we assured of a complete purging of sin? Did we possess the blessed knowledge that we were saved?

Few of us, it is safe to say, possessed by this time any knowledge at all; and yet there were instances when the boldest among us confessed to strange and convincing experiences which even the *Journal* of John Wesley cannot excel. One girl, who has since brought honour upon her native village, declared that a flame of fire played about her head and face as she knelt in prayer. The proverbial bad boy of the community saw, as he rose from his feet, a brilliant red ball roll through the open doorway out into the night. These visions were interpreted by the evangelist of the occasion as proof that the Holy Ghost had, indeed, descended upon one and that the Devil had torn himself from the emancipated soul of the other. Most of us, however, were visited by no such holy manifestations. Too conscience-ridden to feign the presence of Grace when we knew it not, we might have cried with the prophet Isaiah, "We look for salvation, but it is far off from us." "We wait for light but behold obscurity; for brightness but we walk in darkness."

But, saved or not, there was always threatening us the necessity of going home and facing the family. Here it is but fair to say that my own parents did not enter so whole-heartedly into these meetings as did many other heads of homes. My father was, in fact, always singularly disinterested; my mother, herself kept at home by small children, neither discouraged nor encouraged us in our attendance upon them. But we, like all other young people of the village, caught the prevailing excitement and were swept on by it; for, although mob psychology was not so discussed in that day as in this, it was quite as evident and as potent. Indeed, the very unwillingness of my father and mother to place themselves unequivocally among those who laboured for our salvation made our home situation an exceptionally delicate one. For if, touched by some hymn, some fervent appeal, or even by the bravery of our friends and associates, one of us had gone so far as to rise and so much farther as to move forward, such action must be immediately reported at home. Not infrequently the announcement was accomplished by some sympathetic sister while the penitent climbed exhausted and embarrassed to bed to spend an unquiet night in reluctant waiting for the morrow.

One is tempted to state that these mercy-seats

provided for us in our adolescence would have been more crowded had it not been for the awful embarrassment of meeting a family at breakfast. Appearance after punishment was intolerable enough; but it was nothing in comparison with appearance after salvation or an attempt thereto. A hushed air greeted the redeemed as he or she slunk painfully into his seat and with lowered eyes and crimson cheeks proceeded to butter toast or to sugar oatmeal. My father was, I grieve to say, not always guiltless of a half-facetious remark, intended in a kindly spirit but certain to produce confusion. My grandmother, often herself an attendant upon the meetings, was solicitous and curious. My mother, always merciful, was nevertheless vigilant. Her vigilance, however, was a thousand times increased by brothers and sisters who were obviously watching both for signs of regeneration in behaviour or for manifestations of an early fall from grace. Surely the New England restraint and reserve under which so many of us were reared proved totally inadequate to meet such a situation.

Of course, as always, time healed our embarrassment and that of our contemporaries. Some of us, more sure than others of our "calling," joined one church or the other and, once anchored, found ourselves in less turbulent waters. Some, alas! like the foolish and bewitched Galatians, were too soon removed from their profession of faith and the following year, their sufferings having been in vain, became again candidates for a repeated redemption. Time also tempered the vigilance of our families and of our more pious neighbours. Although we were now and then reminded as occasion demanded that our conduct should suggest the fruits of the Spirit in long-suffering, gentleness, and meekness, although we were expected, when testimony was required, to put on the whole armour of God from the girdle of truth to the sword of the Spirit, we passed eleven months of the year in comparative peace and safety.

Time also wrought its changes even in succeeding Januarys. In the early years of the new century one might be accepted as a prospective church member by way of the simpler avenues of decision and desire. Indeed, my youngest brothers and sisters were not required to supply undeniable proofs of that inscrutable and baffling Grace of God, which to my childhood in the nineties, in so far as that childhood had to do with the affairs of the Spirit, lent such perplexity and such undeniable confusion.

PART III

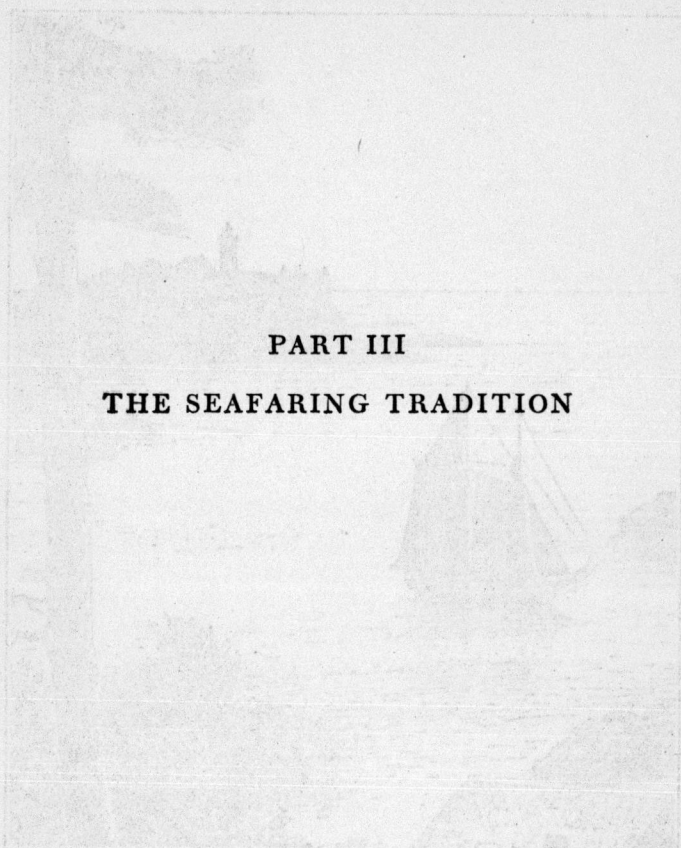

THE SEAFARING TRADITION

CHAPTER I

COAST CHILDREN OF THE NINETIES

(1)

THE heavy toll which change and progress inevitably take as they make their inroads is today nowhere more evident than along the coast of Maine. In the smaller towns and villages even the grass-grown ruins of docks have been destroyed; in the larger, shipbuilding except for the construction of pleasure craft or of an occasional steamship, has virtually ceased. The five- and six-masted schooners, which add a touch of romance to populous harbours like Portland, have floated, rotting, untenanted, and useless, for more than several years. Square-riggers are no more. The lithe and beautiful yachts, which cruise idly from Kittery to Eastport or catch the sun on their brass and mahogany as they lie at anchor about Mount Desert or in Camden harbour, speak all too eloquently of the new industry which feeds and clothes the coast. Maine, once secure in her integrity, depends largely for her livelihood, at least so far as her coast life is concerned, upon the capital of those who seek her shores during the summer months.

In the nineties this was not yet so. True, the tide

of the new prosperity had already crept into the spacious harbours about Mount Desert and Casco. Bar Harbor already knew its millionaires and Old Orchard its many sojourners. But the smaller, more land-locked villages still kept much to themselves, their carpenters building only an occasional cottage for strangers, their small hotels, boarding-houses, and homes entertaining only a few "rusticators." Blue Hill, now deservedly one of the most notable resorts of the coast, knew then neither golf-links nor club-house, neither estates whose clipped lawns sloped to the shore nor Chicago and Cleveland financiers who had money in plenty to spend. And Blue Hill children, although they were occasionally shy before city boys and girls with more stylish clothes and more urbane speech, had the village and the coast for their own.

We knew the manifold excitements of coast life, major and minor. We knew even then the drama of incoming vessels, waiting beyond the Narrows in the outer bay for the tides, tacking up the snug inner channel to anchor just off the harbour island or to tie up at the wharf to unload their provisions for the village stores and to load the staves and larger lumber for their outgoing. The names and the rigging of these craft were as familiar as the words in our spelling-books and far more welcome: *The Gold Hunter*, the *Mildred May*, the *John W. Stetson*. We knew, occasionally, the inexpressible excitement of the arrival of a "foreign ship" from Barbados, manned by strange, swarthy men with bright handkerchiefs around their necks, and in their mouths unintelligible sounds. Once, indeed, as we of our family sat one September evening with our lessons around the dining-room table, such a dark face above such a handkerchief appeared in our open window, its owner muttering outlandish words and gesticulating with tattooed arms and hands. My mother in her perturbation and terror well-nigh threw the lighted lamp at our caller, who, as we discovered upon the hurried arrival of my father, wanted only to know the way to the "medicine house." It was days before we recovered from our fright and more days before we ceased to be the centre of an envious group at school.

We knew and cherished with no little covetousness the stories of the "traders," which had gladdened the hearts of children of an earlier generation. A trader was a vessel from Boston or New York which earned the livelihood of its captain, or perchance of its owner, by carrying annually into the smaller harbours of the coast every kind of ware imaginable and selling its multifarious cargo at prices which the village stores could not meet. Blue Hill children of the sixties and seventies had waited months for the arrival of this floating junk-shop, scanning the sea from every hill and headland for an unfamiliar sail. According to the older people among us, its captain was invariably an accommodating soul, who was not in the least averse to interpreting as coin of the realm any stray bits of old iron, in exchange for which he would proffer oranges and great Boston apples, gorgeously striped candies, dates, figs, and nuts. Moreover, he carried in his hold, for those who had been most thrifty and parsimonious of their small savings, doll buggies and pop-guns, and for the despair of fathers and mothers, who could be lured to the wharf, bolts of cloth and shiny new shoes with voluptuous and alluring tassels.

Sometimes in those days, we understood, still with envy that progress had cheated us of so much greater excitement, Blue Hill had supplied her own traders. An obliging captain, with a weather eye out for his own pocket, sailing light from Boston or New York, Philadelphia or Norfolk, would gladly undertake the filling of commissions in those centres and bring home a sundry cargo. My aunt, a child of the sixties, told us on her infrequent visits the engrossing tale of a new bureau which she procured in this romantic fashion. At the age of six she had pieced together a bed-quilt by the "over and over" method, sewing together innumerable squares and triangles of calico, keeping as she did so the reward for her enterprise and perseverance ever before her eyes. Scanning critically for weeks each distant sail, she at last espied the *Merchant* ploughing through the waters of the outer bay. For hours she waited at the wharf until the tide should be sufficiently favourable for a landing and saw at last her bureau ready for unloading on the quarter-deck. Once again as a reward for industry or virtue (perhaps for both, for in those days, as in our own, they were well-nigh inseparable) she was allowed the fulfilment of great longing. This time, impelled no doubt by her seafaring heritage, she made the choice of a trunk which came after long weeks of waiting by way of another ship, *The Python.*

These shopping sea-captains must, indeed, have been men of gregarious instincts and of great good nature. A slip of paper much torn and obviously incomplete, dated in 1859, gives a partial list of commissions to be fulfilled and suggests the arduous undertaking of the purchaser:

For J. Candage, a hoss harness
For Messrs. Holt, Horton, Candage, & 3 Hinckleys tobaco, both chewing & smoking
For J. C.—a new hat, my own size with 2 cravats & ties
For the minister, one cane, snake's head prefered, not to cost over $1
For Silvester C., a good quantity nails, all sizes, & 12 brass handles
For Coggin family, to invest $20 in white flour & raisins, also nuts of sorts, also toys such as marbles, tops, & a book of pictures
For Miss Clara Wood, stuff for weding dress with threads & silks for sewing same & white lace for triming
For Mrs. Duffy, 1 bolt flowered calico at lowest price, blue & white prefered, also buttons, also wools for kniting socks in bright shades, also pink roses for bonet brims
For Horton boys, 2 large pocket knives

For H. Henderson, 6 steel traps suitable for rabits or foxes

For litle Osgood girl, a doll with black hair, blue eyes, big as possible for $1

For Mrs. Grindle, one singing bird in cage, for the church gift.

Even we in the nineties knew at first hand something of this sort of supply and demand. When I was in the neighbourhood of twelve, my father, together with three other men of the village, bought a quarter share in a two-masted schooner called *The Gold Hunter*. Rumour had it that their act was largely one of charity since the captain and owner had fallen on evil days by the decline of the coast trade. But whatever its cause, the effect brought delighted satisfaction to four large families. *The Gold Hunter* was summarily dispatched to Boston with divers commissions to be accomplished by her relieved captain, and we waited with atavistic feverishness for her return.

Perhaps her cargo, when after a fortnight she again drew to the wharf, was less romantic than those of former days. I am sure, however, that it gave no less thrill. We children of the four families concerned, and we were many, watched with fascination the unloading of barrels of flour, sacks of grain, kegs of molasses and vinegar, cans of pilot bread (that invincible cracker!), bags of oatmeal—all the manifold sorts of provender which were to prove the staples for the men and beasts of our large and respective households during a long winter. We watched, too, the wet line on the black hull of *The Gold Hunter* as it increased in width from her steady rising out of the water during the steady disembowelling of her dark, musty hold.

Most remarkable of all her goods in those relatively fruitless days were crates of oranges, two kegs of white grapes, packed in sawdust, and—most wonderful to relate!—a huge bunch of bananas in a long, slatted frame. It may seem impossible today to wax romantic over a bunch of bananas! But in that huge frame standing on *The Gold Hunter's* deck, behind those masses of brown, tropical grass, were concealed far more than bananas, delectable and desirable as they were in themselves. Therein among those unripe, green protuberances, of whose snug members we caught now and then a baffling glimpse, lay a prestige and a pre-eminence among our fellows which in all the years that have passed I have never been able to recapture. My father had bought the bananas as a surprise. We were all excessively fond of them, but since they were tacitly recognized as an indulgence and since the price of them in the village store, at least of enough to supply our family, was prohibitive, we had never completely satisfied our desire.

The acknowledgment of our supremacy over all the other children in town began as soon as the bananas had been lifted from their frame, cleared of their wiry grass, and hung from a beam in our cellar. Visible from the entrance of our bulkhead, they immediately attracted a crowd of spectators. There was hardly a school-less hour, indeed, for a space of three days, when half a dozen pairs of eyes were not gazing in wonder and envy down those stone stairs. We children meanwhile managed our exhibition by sitting on the open bulkhead doors, swinging our legs and dilating upon our possession with suitable and, I fear, complacent comments.

The culminating moment in this daily-enacted drama occurred one noon when my father, upon inspection of the great ungainly bunch, suggested that we cut the yellowest. That he contemplated any distribution never once occurred to any of us, neither to exhibitors nor to spectators. We watched him procure a box, mount it, and draw his jack-knife from his pocket. I can yet feel the stilling of my heart when he handed down to me, who waited below with outstretched apron, five, six, eight, twelve bananas, when he proposed that we should treat our friends. From that day to this I have never been able to regard a banana with the supercilious stare of the cultivated mind and eye. The munificence and magnanimity of my father, the opulence and distinction of us as a family, remain, always to be evoked by any chance sight of that humblest and ugliest of fruits.

(2)

The minor and usual excitements of coast life were legion. In the nineties there were still among us old sea-captains, barometers of sky and sea, who, in addition to telling us chimerical tales, instructed us in the mysterious ways of weather. We learned to predict the ominous secrets of winds that backed, of restless gulls flying inland, of mare's-tails swishing their milky white across the heavens, of still, cloudless days. We knew what to expect of spring tides, always cherishing the hope that on a March full moon boats would be torn from moorings and lumber floated from the town wharves. We knew when smelts were most likely to "run," coming in great shoals from the outer ocean on night tides in April and May and seeking the tidal streams for spawning. On such nights we went to bed at sundown to be called at three o'clock by my father. Armed with all the pails and baskets of the house, we walked a mile through the darkness to the most favoured brook. The tide was out, and the smelts were foiled and trapped in their tardy return to wider water. Their silver backs and white bellies, as in thousands they hurried pell-mell down the shallow stream, gleamed in the light of our lanterns; and we gathered them in our cold hands by hundreds, filling great baskets full and per-haps, when the miracle was accomplished and we gazed upon our catch, feeling a surprise and exhilara-tion not unlike that of the boy of the Galilean picnic who began his exciting day with but three small fishes.

The offerings of the sea in the ebb of springs were always more momentous than those of ordinary tides. Shells were more plentiful and often more rare.

Wreckage strewed the shores of the outer bay, logs and beams which not infrequently held within their golden brown sides bolts of iron caked with salt. These meant inimitable driftwood fires and were always carried high up the beach and left to dry among the vetches and the lavender. After a spring tide there was also much high talk of treasure and no little search for it. We lived, indeed, on a coast that at once invited and nurtured such fancies. Not far from us lay the very island which was rumoured to hide within its sands the bulk of Captain Kidd's ill-gotten gains. Moreover, not so many years past, two boys who lived near us had been granted an experience, the equal of which few boys of any time or place could boast. Following an old foot-path through the woods during a storm, they had rested against a small boulder beneath a pine tree. One of them, idly kicking the soft mould at the base of the rock, caught the glint of metal, tarnished yet still bright enough to be distinguished against the black earth. They dug farther, with feet and with hands alike, to discover at last an iron pot half filled with gold coins—coins marked by strange designs and a stranger language. They proved to be French pieces of the seventeenth century, probably buried there, so the learned of our coast surmised, by escaping French traders and settlers of the nearby town of Castine when their fort was surprised and captured by the Dutch. What wonder that we scrutinized the wreckage of spring tides and dug now and again in likely coves or beneath giant boulders!

Yet another tale encouraged us to hope for dramatic possibilities even in the ploughing of a spring field. A fisherman not many miles distant had unearthed one May morning, while attempting to cultivate a hitherto barren half-acre, a large piece of copper, marked with unintelligible characters. Seeing in it a remedy for a leaking boat, he tacked it securely to the hull, to be told a few weeks later by summer visitors whom he took out for mackerel, that he had utilized for most practical purposes the corner-stone of a Jesuit chapel, dedicated to Our Lady of Holy Hope in the year 1609!

There was hardly a winter in the nineties when the ocean remained open. By January, sometimes even by Christmas, a great steel-like sheet of ice began to creep farther and farther out toward open sea. Then one cold morning we woke to find no water at all between our shores and those of Long Island, seven miles distant. This meant skating in plenty on the inner bay, and on the outer, once the cold had continued a full week, the laying out of a great track and horse-racing in open sleighs. Not even a launching, which we alas! had been born just too late to see from our own shores, could have been much more thrilling than these village gatherings on certain clear cold afternoons, the participants drawn from village barns, the bells jingling, a blazing fire at the starting-point by which we could warm ourselves with much laughter and many wagers on the horses of our choice.

Those long stretches of ice meant, too, the cutting and hauling of island wood. Oxen drew the creaking sledges which smelled of pine and fir, and obliging farmers encouraged us, once we had obtained our parents' consent, to ride out empty and to return on the top of the load or clinging to the broad runners. The white expanse stretched far and wide beneath a clear, cold sky. The islands were surrounded by rough, uneven boundaries where the tide had cracked and broken the ice, throwing up jagged slabs and cakes around their edges. Wraiths of blue mist rose from the muzzles of the oxen above the icicles clinging to their hairy throats; the creaking of the sledges was now and then supplemented by the booming of the ice as the moving water far beneath it raised or lowered the great solid mass. The climatic changes, even of thirty years, have robbed the coast children of today of no higher adventure.

More suddenly even than it had come, the great sheet of ice broke up and moved seaward. Suspicious gleams of pale blue appeared here and there on a warm, windy morning in March or early April; sullen and explosive muttering punctuated the air. Then with the full outgoing tide the cakes of ice began to move, jamming and hurtling one another, sometimes being thrown into the air by the pressure beneath. Adventuresome boys of parents more careless than our own occasionally tried the risky experiment of crossing the inner bay by jumping from one to another if perchance the break-up occurred on a Saturday. If it happened on ordinary days, it must be intermittently watched from the schoolhouse windows, which on one side faced the sea, but which were placed so high in the wall as to be barely accessible even to the most ambitious vision. The difficulty of keeping one's mind and eyes upon one's books on such a morning was intense.

Tuesdays, Thursdays, and Saturdays in spring and summer were fish-boat mornings. By seven o'clock on days when the tide served, Captain Andrew Cole had sailed from the outer bay, having far earlier hauled his trawl. The young representatives of each family table gathered at the wharf, not reluctant to wait their turn while the green water slapped at the piers and the gulls were certain of full stomachs. A five-pound haddock, cleaned and scraped, could be bought for fifteen cents, the black stripe down his silvery sides guaranteeing wary purchasers against the despised hake, which no Maine connoisseur of fish could tolerate. There were clams, too, dipped from a sodden tub at ten cents a quart measure and, upon occasion, tinker mackerel in ravishing shades of blue and green, so cheap that two dozen might be bought without greatly diminishing the family pocket-book.

There were clams to be dug from the mud flats, many bare feet spotting them by the tiny jets of water which they spouted from their hiding-places.

The backaches produced by heavy clam-hoes in tough mud were always less painful than those engendered by piling wood or cultivating garden rows of potatoes or beans! We baked them by building fires of driftwood beneath flat rocks and laying the clams between layers of wet seaweed. Nearly every summer these clambakes took on a co-operative character participated in by the village at large. On these occasions our elders chartered a schooner in the harbour large enough to consider a hundred persons a mere handful. We sailed then to Long Island, laden with foodstuffs sufficient for any ordinary siege, and spent the day on wider, sandier shores. The dinner served on such village picnics tested the gastronomic capacities of the community and could hardly be excelled by any eighteenth century repast. Lobsters and clams, broiled and baked, fish in chowders, hard-boiled eggs, sandwiches and doughnuts, fresh cakes, turnovers, and tarts, blueberry and apple pies, root beer, lemonade and coffee! What wonder that the sail homeward before a southeast wind was silent and that we trudged in families, still silent, up the village street, filled, among many other things, with a sleepy content!

(3)

Beyond all these tangible influences, the coast itself, and the very fact that we lived upon it, placed its intangible mark upon our minds. Secure though we were in our safe haven, we knew full well that the sea was treacherous and insecure. Something of the same shrewd, patient wisdom must be the heritage of prairie children or of those dwelling by great rivers, who are born to scent disaster in rising winds and waters. Few of us of my generation will ever forget that tragic November night when the Boston boat went down with all on board. Reared on tales of shipwreck and suffering upon oceans near and far, we were not surprised by the hardships which every winter brought within our knowledge. We read or were told of lighthouse children drowned by falling into fissures of the rock, of a woman who tended a great lamp through a three days' storm while the body of her husband lay in the lighthouse sitting-room. We knew of outlying islands beset with starvation in an especially bitter winter, of mailboats foundered in high seas. Is it too much then to believe that there crept into our minds earlier than into the minds of most children a sense of the inevitability, not only of suffering but of endurance as well, that we grew, perhaps unconsciously and insensibly, to look upon sorrow not as an individual, concrete matter but rather as a mighty abstraction, necessary and common to all human life? An easier, more fortified age may well question such an assumption; but few who were born to a seafaring heritage and few who knew coast life even a quarter of a century ago will doubt it.

CHAPTER II

GEOGRAPHY WITHOUT GEOGRAPHIES

IN the nineties we children of the village school cherished and nurtured a kind of lofty patronage toward geographies and their authors. In the first place, the required memorizing of certain definitions with which our geography began, in no sprightly fashion, seemed to us absurd and useless.

"An island is any body of land, large or small, which is completely surrounded by water."

"A bay is an arm of the sea extending into the land."

"A strait is a narrow passage of water connecting two larger bodies of water."

"A cape is a point of land, often precipitous and dangerous, extending into the ocean."

What need had we to learn by heart such a dull and lifeless definition of an island, which, if we did not recite it in exactly the words of the geography, entailed staying after school and copying it fifty times on our slates? Had we not long known, from far more dramatic recitals than these, Martinique with its hurricanes and Mozambique on its coral reefs? We lived on a bay and sailed a dozen times each summer through a strait. As for capes, our very grandparents had rounded the Horn in all weathers and in all seasons, had known the Cape of Good Hope far better than Cape Porpoise or Cape Split.

In the second and more important place, the maker of the one geography we knew always failed us in his description of the most interesting portions of the world; in fact, we could have furnished him with any number of stray bits of information wherewith to embellish and to heighten his pages.

"Cadiz," wrote he, "is the most important seaport of Southern Spain, located not far from the famous Strait of Gibraltar. It has long been noted for its foreign trades. Its chief products for export are silks, fruits, wines, and coral."

Now I myself knew Cadiz far better than I knew the village of North Penobscot seven miles away. I could have told that author many things. My grandfather had voyaged again and again to Cadiz; my grandmother had spent months on end in that most fascinating of cities while her husband had sailed through the Straits, across the Mediterranean, through the Red Sea and the Arabian to India, thence to China. I could have told him that Cadiz was one of the oldest cities in all the world; that King Solomon, indeed, had traded there, bringing back therefrom to Jerusalem ivory for his temple and apes and peacocks for the amusement of his many wives. I knew, if he did not, that Cadiz was a white city on an island, secured against the ravages of the sea by a great white wall. From the deck of my grandfather's

ship at anchor in its wide harbour on a moonlight
night Cadiz, with its snowy domes and spires, looked
like nothing so much as a mammoth white flower
floating on the sea. And surely in his brief and stilted
sentences he suggested nothing of the gaiety of
Cadiz! In my grandmother's day there had been
much drinking of wine in Spanish gardens filled with
oleanders and magnolias, music at night from Spanish cavaliers in plumed hats, with guitars carelessly
slung on coloured cords about their shoulders. There
had been dancing to the sound of tambourines and
castanets; and in the long evening señoritas in gay
shawls had paced the many terraces of Cadiz accompanied by señors, who languidly twirled red roses in
their white teeth. With lamentable lack of imagination the geography gave us no picture of Cadiz,
choosing rather to include one of the Royal Park in
Madrid, which was not on the seacoast at all and
interested none of us with "its cool, healthful climate,
justly prized in a hot country."

I hated, too, the simple questions which the geographer placed at the end of his account and which
must be answered in complete sentences and in his
identical words on pain of penalty.

"What is the most important seaport of Southern
Spain?" "Where is it located?" "For what has it long
been noted?" "What are its chief products?"

Other children, too, had other and equal griev-
ances against him. One family felt bitterly his neglect of Martinique.

"Martinique," he wrote, "is a rich island of the West Indies fifty miles in length and contains a population of nearly 150,000 persons, nine-tenths of whom are mulattoes and blacks. It produces sugar, coffee, cotton, and indigo. The principal places are Fort France, St. Peters, and Trinity."

It must be admitted that such a lifeless estimation as this was extremely exasperating to those whose ancestors had weathered in the harbour of St. Peters the devastating Martinique hurricane of 1831! They looked in vain for some mention of those great stalks of sugar cane which for days converted the waters about St. Peters into a Sargasso Sea, of those innumerable black corpses which strewed the shores until they were burned in mammoth trenches.

Our disappointment might have been somewhat alleviated had our teacher encouraged us to supplement the geography. But, unfortunately for us in this respect at least, the instruction in our day did not embolden one to additional comments. We learned the lesson as it was assigned us, and any remarks of our own were adjudged neither pertinent nor valuable.

Lastly, the geographer's maps were a constant source of irritation. He was sufficiently accurate when it came to the United States and territories, to us the least interesting of any of his sections. We memorized and recited these according to his divisions, the New England States, the Middle Atlantic, North and South Atlantic, Middle Western, etc. The capi-

tals must be placed inextricably in our minds from
Harrisburg and Tallahassee to Oklahoma City and
Sacramento. Not one was held to be an honourable
point of ignorance! But when he was confronted with
the richer and more pleasant task of providing us
with foreign maps—and it never once occurred to us
that he did not himself with his own wilful mind and
hand execute his own drawings—he again was found
wanting. For example, he gave only the most miserable corner on the map of North America to the
island of Greenland. This he presented as extending
from the Arctic circle in a loop of pale pink. Conde-
scending to name only a few of the more important
places on the coast, he entirely omitted what was to
us the most significant. We knew that not far from
Cape Farewell on the extreme southern point was a
sound called Christian Sound. Did he take the trouble to name this dramatic spot or even to indent his
wavy coastline to suggest its turbulent waters? He
did not. We knew that in the spring of the year huge
icebergs floated west of Iceland, down the Straits of
Denmark, past Cape Farewell and into Christian
Sound. We knew these things from the hair-raising
tale of one who had himself traversed these wild
seas.

This captain, blown north from the Banks of New-
foundland in the year 1869 and finding in these unfamiliar waters better fishing than he had ever
known, continued still farther north until he was
within sight of the forbidding coast of Greenland.

Small as was his ship and fraught with dangers as had already been his voyage, he was still adventuresome. Determining to land, he lay to one night waiting for daybreak only to find himself at dawn in the midst of ice such as he had never seen. According to his doubtless much-embellished tale, he was surrounded by a squadron of ships of ice. They towered above his puny schooner, some crowned with snow, some clear green with the sun shining through them as through empty glass bottles. In that these great bergs all resembled craft of various cuts, he saw the work of the Devil reproving him for his own hardihood. His hair assumed the familiar whiteness we had always known on that awful morning of manœuvring among and between these gigantic Arctic vessels. To increase his confusion, giant birds of strange plumage and frightful, raucous cries flew above his masts, making the skies hideous with their uproar. His final escape he attributed not to any skill of his own, but to the blessed nearness of Christian Sound, the very holy name of which caused the ships of ice to turn southward in their course and at last to disappear.

The geographer brought upon himself still greater scorn by another and even less forgivable omission. Lying northeast of the harbour of Shanghai—a harbour familiar to practically all descendants of foreign seafarers—and in the wide and greedy mouths of the river Yangtze-kiang is the island of Tsung Ming. To credit the geographer with the scant justice due him, it is but fair to say that he had included in his map the bare outlines of this important place. But that he had seen fit to engrave no name upon its dull green surface was an inexcusable offence in the condemnation of which the whole school joined.

For the island of Tsung Ming was inextricably connected with our own village. Certain events of the late fifties which had occurred therein were woven and interwoven into the very tissue of our life and thought. The Governor of that island and two hundred and fifty of his most bloodthirsty subjects had in the fifties been foiled by the intrepidity and the genius of a Blue Hill sailor, at that time a mere boy, later Captain R. G. F. Candage of Brookline, Massachusetts.

Even then first mate in spite of his youth, he had been shipwrecked in a terrific storm on a reef off Tsung Ming, the barque being literally broken in two by the force of the awful impact with the rocks. His captain had placed him in command of the longboat with a crew of twenty-four, he himself embarking with eight men in a smaller, and each setting out for Shanghai. The boats became separated, the more heavily laden long-boat finally landing on the coast of Tsung Ming, which the mate at first mistook for the mainland. Not a little disquieted by the almost immediate arrival of a band of Chinese armed with pikes, he succeeded in bribing one of their number with Mexican gold to guide him to the ruler or governor of the island from whom he might ask assistance in the shape of a junk, for he realized his boat was not to be trusted with its cargo of twenty-four men and their necessary effects.

Of that silent, threatening walk across Tsung Ming under a broiling August sun we had been often told. It was five miles to the governor's house. A negro cook and a steward accompanied the mate and his sullen guide, their black faces and curly heads attracting much attention and more suspicion as they passed through the small island villages.

Once they had reached their destination and had been received by the governor in a large open room of his mansion, difficulties appeared insufferable. "Taow-tai," the Chinese word for ruler, had, together with signs and money, been sufficient to secure an interview. But when it was discovered that there was no means whatever of further communication between the Blue Hill sailor and the ruler of Tsung Ming, matters rapidly assumed a portentous character.

It was obvious, too, as we understood, that from the start the governor was none too favourably inclined toward his guests. His unintelligible mutterings to the guide and the dark look which steadily grew upon his yellow face lent Mr. Candage small hope. Signs proved useless. The governor wrote a few words in Chinese and handed them to the distressed mate; the mate wrote a few words in English and handed them to the governor. The guide exhibited his gold coin to the crowd that had gathered, conveying, with his act, the impression to Mr. Candage that more was about to be demanded. The situation became pregnant with thwarted possibilities and imminent probabilities. Finally the governor, apparently pricked by his lack of hospitality, ordered a watermelon to be brought and served to his guests. As they ate, the door communicating with the women's apartment slowly opened, interested faces appeared, curiosity and excitement mounted, until one of the Tsung Ming ladies, unable longer to preserve even a relative decorum, ran across the room and passed her hand through the black wool of the terrified cook.

But also as they ate, an idea began to form itself in the shrewd, practical mind of the Yankee sailor, the State of Maine began to pit her native intelligence against that of China. Upon the table before Mr. Candage lay the pieces of rind and the oval black seeds of the watermelon. Glancing for the last time into the sceptical, unyielding face of the ruler of Tsung Ming, he took a piece of the rind, quickly fashioned it with his pocket knife into the rude hull of a ship, and stuck three matches into it for masts. From two smaller pieces of rind he carved the boats, which together with thirty-four seeds he placed on his watermelon ship. On the left of the table to represent the position of the reef off Tsung Ming he piled helter-skelter other rinds to serve as dangerous rocks. Then, while the governor and the crowd of spectators watched from doors and windows as well as from within the room, he suddenly ran his ship upon the reef and broke it in halves.

He was conscious of breathless attention and more conscious of a more sympathetic attitude. But he was not yet done. Still apparently oblivious of his host, he launched his two boats from the wrecked ship. Into the larger, the long-boat, he placed twenty-four seeds, one by one arranging them so that the onlookers could see that the boat was overcrowded, moved it slowly across the table from the reef, and said in a loud voice "Tsung Ming." Into the smaller he placed eight seeds, moved it across the table, let it fall to the floor and sadly shook his head and said "Shanghai" in a solemn voice as he did so.

That the ruler of Tsung Ming understood these proceedings was immediately evident. It was evident, too, that his feeling toward his American guest had changed. He had recognized a man more clever than himself and was willing to admit it. More food was brought; offers of further hospitality were unmistakably made; and strange and courteous salutations of respect were accorded the shipwrecked men. But Mr. Candage could waste no time. Had he not left, we always asked ourselves at this point, twenty-one men five miles away who for all he knew might already have fallen prey to Chinese pirates and pikemen?

Drawing a Mexican dollar from his pocket, he held it to view, spreading his hands as he did so and asking the question, "Shanghai?" Some supplementary conversation ensued between the guide and the governor. Obviously his request was understood. The ruler of Tsung Ming raised the dollar, laid it again on the table, and then slowly counted to ten on his fingers. For ten dollars he would take the ship-wrecked men to Shanghai. Delightedly he, too, resorted to melon rinds and seeds, showing therewith that his ship should carry ten men as a crew and that the long-boat should be safely taken in tow.

The bargain struck, he accompanied the mate, cook, steward and somewhat disgruntled guide by junk to the shore where the long-boat had landed. There he angrily dissembled his treacherous subjects, now swelled to two hundred and glowering upon the boat, which had been earlier in the day launched in haste and which held twenty-one excited and frightened sailors at a safe distance.

Shanghai was reached in safety and in friendship. The captain and his eight men had already arrived in the smaller boat, and great rejoicing ensued. Who knows what international spirit had not been cemented by this courageous and ingenious seizure of fortune, conceived and executed by a Blue Hill mind with the assistance of a Chinese watermelon? And who will wonder at our indignation against that unconscious geographer who had failed to inscribe by name an island so favoured and so justly notorious? [1]

[1] This story of a bargain by melon seeds was told by Capt. R. G. F. Candage of Blue Hill, Maine, and of Brookline, Massachusetts, to the late Mr. Charles Boardman Hawes and by him especially adapted for use in Chapters XX and XXI of his story *The Mutineers*, published in 1920 by the Atlantic Monthly Press, Boston.

CHAPTER III

A BOY'S FIRST VOYAGE IN 1856

IN my childhood a day's excursion, whether by land or by sea, was rarely planned without expert advice concerning the weather. This we or our parents obtained from the brain and the barometer of Captain Edgar Stevens, who lived high upon a hill overlooking the bay and the open ocean. He could calculate almost to an hour a change in wind or water. He was an engaging old man living alone during his last years in his big white house and surrounded on afternoons and evenings by many books and papers. In the mornings he did his housework. He was the despair even of our most painstaking mothers, for he kept his large rooms as shipshape as he had ever kept the decks and cabins of his vessel.

He had had a varied life at sea beginning with his early boyhood. His first voyage at the age of fifteen in the year 1856 held always a favourite place in our ears. When he was nearing seventy and I had finished college, I induced him to write the story of it for me, hoping that he might be able to place upon paper something of the stirring quality of his own speech. I was not disappointed. In his narrative he provides an interesting commentary on the educa-

tional powers of such a relatively school-less life as
his, spent instead under the relentless tutelage of the
sea. I give his account precisely as he wrote it for me,
copying it from his accurate and closely written
pages. There is, indeed, no need to correct his spelling or to improve upon his construction:

.   .   .   .

I will most cheerfully give you the narrative of
my first voyage.

The ship's name was *Louis Napoleon* hailing from
New York. She was two thousand tons burthen,
meaning her cargo capacity. She was a new ship,
built in Baltimore and loading there when I joined
her. Her master was Captain Judah Chase of Blue
Hill.

We sailed from Annapolis Roads, December 20th,
1855, bound to Liverpool, England, with a full
cargo of wheat and flour. The crew consisted of
thirty-four seamen, six boys including the captain's
son, Harry Chase, and myself, a carpenter, a carpenter's mate, a bo'sun, a cook, a steward, and a first,
second, and third mate. We had good weather and
favourable winds, and the ship proved speedy.

On January 6th, 1856, indications of bad weather
appeared. The barometer commenced to fall rapidly;
the wind died to a dead calm; the surface of the
ocean had not a ripple nor did the ship have steerage
way. Our position was in mid-ocean and about five
hundred miles from the Azores or Western Islands.

I shall never forget that day. There was something weird, uncanny in the air. There was not a breath of wind, the ocean a mirror, the noble ship gracefully rising and falling to the swell, the immense sails hanging listlessly from the yards and threshing against the masts with every motion of the vessel. Still the day was fine, bright and sunny. But that ever faithful barometer said, "Something doing soon! Lookout! Prepare!"

The captain was on the alert. To use the late phrase, he sat up, took notice, and began to do business right away. His first order was, "Call all hands and shorten sail." Then occurred a busy and exciting scene. Every man responded to the call with the utmost alacrity, each striving to outdo another in the various duties called into action by the order. Even the man at the helm was ordered to join the rest of the crew, and Harry and I were sent to the wheel to hold it steady, no very hard task as it was dead calm and no steerage way on the ship. In a very short time the sail was reduced to three close-reefed topsails and fore-topmast-staysail. How strange it seemed to see that ship under so little sail in a dead calm on an apparently fine day! But the barometer was still falling, falling, a warning not to be by any means disregarded. The next order was to put extra lashings on all things movable on deck, spare spars, water-casks, boats, chicken-coops, everything likely to be washed away; and it was late in the afternoon when the crew had finished doing all these things.

Soon the appearance of the sky changed. Dark

clouds began to gather with lurid streaks between them. The sun was obscured from view; the clouds changed to inky blackness; the swell of the ocean increased in size and ripples began to appear. Low moans of wind could be heard through the ship's rigging and spars, causing the ship to feel her helm; the yards were quickly braced up, and the ship brought to on the starboard tack. In short order we got the full force of the wind preceded by a squall of rain and sleet, which made it impossible to look to windward. She headed up to the sea pretty well, and the heavy canvas held, although it was subjected to such an enormous strain.

Night came on, and the darkness was intense. The gale had now stirred up a tremendous sea; the waves ran high and occasionally broke over the bow of the ship, flooding the decks with water. Still everything held, and she was making fairly good weather of it. Under the conditions then prevailing, we would have weathered the gale all right, and the final catastrophe would not have occurred. But it was fated otherwise.

As the night wore on, the gale increased to hurricane force. One after another the sails were blown from the bolt-ropes. First went the main topsail, followed by the fore and mizzen and fore-topmast-staysail. The ship, thus relieved of her canvas, fell off into the trough and commenced to roll fearfully, shipping big seas and filling the decks with water. One such sea, boarding the ship about midships, smashed in the galley doors and washed the poor coloured cook out and overboard. No mortal power could save him! Now the ship became utterly unmanageable, and in consequence the lofty spars, that is, the topmasts and topgallant-masts, went by the board, together with all the yards, and lay in the water to leeward, one huge, mixed, tangled mass of wreckage, which being still attached by the backstays, threatened to smash in the side of our now dismantled vessel. Nothing remained standing but the three lower masts, the fore, main, and mizzen. About midnight the mizzen went, breaking off close to the deck.

But when it went over the side, it did not drift away because of the rigging which held it. It was, therefore, another course of danger, for in that raging sea that immense spar would come up under the counter of the ship with the force of a battering-ram, threatening to knock a hole through that part. At last after repeated tuggings the chain bolts to which the rigging was attached drew out from the side of the ship, and the spar drifted away.

Meanwhile the ship began to leak. The carpenter on sounding the pumps found more than four feet of water in the hold. The forward deck-house which quartered the crew was smashed by the sea; and the sailors came rushing into the cabin pell-mell, completely panic-stricken, some praying, some groaning, others laughing and swearing—all in a most helpless state. Previously the captain had been badly injured by being crushed between two spars floating on deck and carried to his stateroom, suffering much pain.

Sending now for the officers, he told them to get some sense into that crazy crew, to get them organized into gangs of eight men each, and man the pumps. He commanded further to impress upon their minds that unless the ship was freed of water, she would founder, and all hands would go to Davy Jones's locker together. The second mate and carpenter, two big strong men, the best in the ship, after much persuasion and no little thumping, made those madmen understand what was required of them. Each man was provided with a life-line to lash himself to the wooden bitts surrounding the pumps; and eight of them with two officers started out into that turmoil of rushing waters, inky blackness, and howling gale. They had a hard time of it, being frequently engulfed in the big seas that came over the rail and would have been washed overboard had they not been lashed to the bitts. At the end of half an hour they were relieved by another gang, and so it went on during that long, frightful night, the pumps never stopping.

You can imagine that I was having quite a sea experience for a fifteen-year-old boy. Harry and I took our turn at the pumps with the rest. Still I was not frightened, only mighty uncomfortable, being soaking wet to the skin as were all the others. And I did wish more than once that I was at home!

Daylight came at last. What a sight it revealed! A wild waste of angry waters, lashed into fury by the gale which had not in the least abated, the waves running to alarming heights, and that sky which seemed to be right down upon us, angry, forbidding, pitiless. A glance over the deck was appalling. Could it be possible that this noble fabric of yesterday was reduced to such a wreck? Stripped of her sails, yards, and spars, her rails and bulwarks gone, only one boat left, a tangled mass of ropes and gear encumbering the broken top timbers fore and aft, the once gallant *Louis Napoleon* lay rolling, wallowing in those mighty billows!

We were cheered and encouraged, however, when the carpenter reported, upon sounding the pumps soon after daylight, that we were gaining on the leak. Then all hands had a better heart to work, and hope revived. It was long towards noon when the barometer began to show an upward movement; and before night the wind had moderated a good deal. Still the sea ran high, and the ship was necessarily making bad weather of it as we had no means or place to set a stitch of canvas to steady her.

Captain Chase under the ministrations of the steward and with the help of the contents of the medicine-chest commenced to improve. His pain subsided in a great measure, and he was soon much more comfortable. Fortunately no bones were broken.

In the early morning of the second day the American ensign was set Union-down on the stump of the main-mast as a signal of distress; and all during the day we scanned the horizon eagerly in the hope of seeing a sail. The long hours wore on, pumps still going and gradually gaining on the leak. At night the gale had greatly moderated, but the sea continued very high, at times breaking over the ship.

On the morning of the third day, January 9th, the pumps sucked, thus signifying that the ship was dry; the force of the wind reduced to a moderate gale; the sea became smoother. We took off the after-hatch and began throwing cargo overboard in order to lighten the after part of the ship; and in a few hours the surface of the ocean was covered with barrels of flour bobbing up and down in the sea. In the afternoon the welcome sound of "Sail-ho!" rang out, and in a short time a ship could be seen to windward, steering directly for us. A ship under full sail at sea is always a fine sight. But on this occasion it was doubly so as it meant deliverance from our sore straits.

After coming within hailing distance, her captain hailed us. Captain Chase, who was now able to be on deck, answered, giving our ship's name and some brief particulars of our condition and telling him distinctly that we wanted to be taken off the wreck. The ship, which proved to be the *Alfred Stover*, of Waldoboro, Maine, from New York bound to Liverpool, kept on her course, after speaking to us, for about a half a mile or less and hove to. That is, her captain brought her up to wind with the main-topsail aback so that the ship remained at a standstill excepting the drift she made. As the sea was running very high and no boat could live in it, we supposed her captain was going to stand by us until the sea went down enough so that it would be safe for them to lower a boat and board us. Hence all hands got busy making preparations to leave the wreck. The crew were ordered each one to make up a small bag of clothing. Such a thing as taking our sea-chests along was impossible. All was excitement and intense relief; and we kept our eyes alternately on ship and sea, anxiously waiting for signs of moderation in wind and water so that a boat might safely be launched.

Imagine then our utter astonishment and dismay when at the expiration of an hour, we saw the ship square her yards and keep on her course. The wind was fair for her and blowing hard, and soon she was hull down and out of sight. It is impossible to describe our bitter disappointment and our intense indignation. The maledictions hurled by the different members of the crew after that captain who had deserted us should most effectually have wiped him off the face of the earth or the sea! His leaving us was a most inhuman act. I am glad to say I heard of none like it during many years at sea. Apparently he did not care to be bothered with saving human lives as he had a fine, fair wind and wanted to make a quick passage!

That night and the next day and night passed in much the same manner, our disappointment, however, making the situation even more desperate. The *Louis Napoleon* rolled and wallowed in the seas, which now were beginning to go down a little. We still had to keep the pumps going at intervals in order to keep the ship free of water. Occasionally we would get some sunshine. Fortunately the galley fire was going all the time, and we had plenty to eat. No more hardtack for us! We had flour galore and to spare, having thrown overboard already a few thousand barrels. In the cargo was a small shipment of grape fruit, some three or four hundred barrels, which we came upon when we were throwing the flour overboard. We feasted right royally on that rare luxury!

The morning of the fifth day dawned showing a leaden sky and a dreary waste of waters, sea making, and indications of more bad weather. Anxious eyes were eagerly scanning the horizon, hoping and hoping for the welcome sight of a sail. All on board, even we boys, realized that another gale must send us to the bottom. At last my own eyes riveted themselves to a wee speck on the distant horizon which looked like the top-gallant-sail of a ship. I watched and waited, the captain's son at my side. It *was* a sail! Soon her topsails came into view and then her hull. She was to windward of us, and we knew she must see us, for she altered her course and steered directly for us.

When she was within hailing distance, her captain spoke to us. Captain Chase replied asking to be taken off the wreck. The ship proved to be the *John J. Boyd* from Liverpool, England, bound to New York and commanded by Captain Austin. She carried nearly six hundred steerage passengers, Mormons, whose destination was Salt Lake City. The ship was hove to within safety distance from us; a life-boat was lowered and in charge of the first officer boarded us. Mr. Woodward, for that was his name, on getting on board took in the situation at once. He and Captain Chase recognized each other as old acquaintances and former shipmates for they had voyaged together some years before. They soon made their plans. He was to take one load of our men to the rescuing ship. While he was gone, we were to get our only boat left, the long boat, a fine large one, which had fortunately escaped destruction, into the water. Upon his return both boats could take the balance of the officers and the crew. This was accordingly done, Captain Chase being the last to leave the ship. The sea was running very high, and the greatest skill and seamanship were required in managing and steering the boats to prevent their being swamped. As it was, the spray flew over us drenching us all.

The view of our once splendid *Louis Napoleon* as we looked at her from the boats was pathetic, indeed. Rising and falling on those immense waves, now poised on the crest of one, now almost hid from sight in the trough of another, she drifted, abandoned and alone! How long would it be, we asked ourselves, before she was swallowed by the insatiable ocean? Not very long. The deserted pumps will end her story soon. She probably foundered that same night

or soon thereafter. Certain it is that she was never
reported as being sighted by any passing vessel.

It was rather a difficult job to board the *John J.
Boyd* as the sea was of so rough and treacherous a
nature. As our boat was such a good one, it was decided to save it rather than cast it adrift. Accordingly
it was hoisted in on deck and the life-boat was hoisted
up and stowed in its proper place.

The *John J. Boyd* was an emigrant ship plying between New York and Liverpool. She belonged to
the Black Ball line of packets and was owned in New
York. Even in 1856 there were very few ocean
steamships, and any one then prophesying that such
greyhounds as the *Mauretania* and *Lusitania* would
ever be built would have been considered mad. The
Boyd was expressly fitted for carrying steerage passengers, or emigrants. The whole of the between-
decks was utilized for that purpose, being fitted with
accommodations for six to eight hundred people,
while the lower hold was used for cargo. She was a
good-sized ship, about twelve hundred tons, and besides the officers carried a crew of twenty-five men.

I shall never forget the condition of that crew.
About one-third of them were totally unfit for duty
because of sickness, frost bite, scurvy, and bad usage.
Those Black Ball packets were notorious in the fifties
for ill usage and brutality on the part of captains and
officers. It was a godsend to those sailors to be recruited by the addition of our crew. Darkness had

fallen by the time the extra hands were told off into the regular watches, and, with the night, came the expected bad weather. The wind increased to a gale, making it necessary to close-reef the topsails. With the wind came snow and sleet and bitter cold.

I was in the watch on deck that first night from eight until midnight. Little difference did it make that I was a boy and that I was half sick from five days of fear and exposure. I had to stand out and take all that was coming to me just the same as the men. That was going on sixty years ago, but I have not forgotten the cold and snow and headache of that awful night.

Life on the *John J. Boyd* was anything but pleasant. Our quarters were worse than crowded, and the food furnished us was something awful. Salt junk and hardtack were the principal items on the bill of fare. The former looked like a piece of mahogany, and that is what the sailors used to call it. On the *Boyd* when we were cutting off slices for our dinner, one of us would sing,

Old horse, old horse, what brought you here?

Then all would peal out the answer given by the ghost of the old horse,

I've carted stone for many a year
From Sacarap to Portland Pier.
Now that I'm dead from sheer abuse,
I'm salted down for sailors' use.

Nor was our comfort increased by the weather. Gale followed gale. Some of these were fair, but for the most of the time westerly winds prevailed which were against us. After two weeks I was taken down with the ship fever, which disease was prevalent among the passengers. For days I lay in my narrow bunk, completely unconscious. Finally the ship's doctor brought me around again, all right but very weak. I was told by my shipmates how forty of the passengers had died on the passage and how they were buried at sea. No day without its burial over the side. Often, indeed, there were two.

At last one morning the welcome sound of the anchor chain running through the hawsepipe aroused me as I lay in my bunk. Exerting what little strength I possessed, I pulled myself up and looked out of the little window above me. There was the lowland of Sandy Hook at the entrance to New York harbour. Never in my long life has there been a sight so grateful to my eyes as that! Soon a tugboat hailed us, and the *John J. Boyd* was taken in tow up the harbour and docked in New York. Thirty-five days had passed since we were taken off the wreck. We arrived in New York on the 18th of February, 1856.

When I reached Blue Hill a week later, I was a much weaker and wiser boy than when I had left the previous November. But thin and pale as I was, the sea had somehow gotten into my blood, and after a month of my mother's cooking, I was ready to start off again.

I may say in conclusion to my story that the hurricane of January 6th, 1856, was a memorable one. It swept the North Atlantic Ocean, and proved the death of many ships besides the *Louis Napoleon* and the loss of many lives.

CHAPTER IV

MY GRANDFATHER'S WRECK OFF
IRELAND

I NEVER knew my grandfather in the flesh. He died a year before my birth. But I knew him in his spirit which stared at me from his deepset eyes and his thin, much-lined face in my grandmother's room. I knew him, too, from the many stories of him which her fervent, cherishing nature did not allow us for one moment to forget.

He was born in 1823, one of a large family, the five sons of which all followed the sea as had their fathers before them. Early, and apparently eagerly, released from school, he began at sixteen his arduous profession. At twenty-six, after a series of disastrous experiences which would have left lines on any face, he was master of his own ship and of the fate of others as well as of himself.

He was apparently a stern, silent man. Perhaps, indeed, we had fared slim had it been left to *him* to recount his adventures. Above these, in many ports and on every sea, towered always the terrible experience of his wreck off Ireland in 1847. I cannot remember when this tale was first told to me, when I did not know and treasure its every detail. It seemed to have been born with all of us, like our hands and our feet. At that time he was first mate of a barque, the *Sarah E. Snow*, owned by a Boston shipping firm, mastered by a Blue Hill captain and manned by a Blue Hill crew. The last of that crew to sign up was my grandfather's favourite brother, he taking at the latest moment the position of second mate—a position suddenly left vacant by a certain superstitious Mr. Hause, who lived to congratulate himself upon the validity of his premonitions. The *Sarah E. Snow*, sailing from New York on the 3rd day of January, was laden with corn for Ireland, which was already suffering from the beginnings of the great famine of 1848. From the day of sailing the captain was a prey to gloomy forebodings and made no secret of his conviction that the ship would never reach shore. That his melancholy sentiments in any way affected his seamanship was never suggested to us. Doubtless there was no connection between the two. But we knew full well all those catastrophic happenings which began on the 24th of January in a perilous gale off the coast of Galway.

Laying to in that frightful wind, the *Sarah E. Snow* was struck by a heavy sea which knocked her on her beam ends and drowned the forecastle watch. The same sea, rushing into the cabin, drowned the captain and well-nigh finished my grandfather, also. In his own concise words a crew of twenty-nine men were "swished off" and out of sight, except for three on the quarter-deck, my grandfather, his brother (the second mate) and one other. Another sea took the second mate in its cruel wake, and in less than half an hour my grandfather was left alone.

For four days he drifted on the wrecked ship, expecting every conscious moment to join his companions below. He had no food or water. Once, falling into an exhausted sleep, he awoke to find the rope with which he had lashed himself just slipping its knots. On the morning of the 28th, waking again to a feverish consciousness, he saw that he was but four miles from a surf-beaten island coast.

"Little comfort in that sight!" repeated my grandmother's dramatic, sepulchral voice. "He knew full well that the breakers would prove his doom."

But the island, only a few miles from Galway, contained intrepid, if hungry, peasants, who launched a rude craft and rescued him in the very nick of time. For the ill-omened *Sarah E. Snow* struck the rocks and in the first sea was turned bottom up!

Slightly less harrowing than those four days on the wreck was the tale of my grandfather's terrible, delirious fever in the hut of some kindly peasants. He lay for a fortnight more dead than alive in the crib of the family cow, she being utilized to give him greater warmth as she stood above his bed. In the home of those who were themselves starving there was little enough for a sick man. But they suffered still further in giving him what they had; and during my childhood my grandmother was still voicing her gratitude and admiration. Partially recovered, he saw to it that the American consul on the mainland was informed of his condition, whereupon he became acquainted with a different mode of life. For he was taken to the ancestral castle of an Irish nobleman who entertained him right royally until he was able to go home.

It was in April that he once more reached New York and shipped north on a Maine schooner. Already the news of the *Sarah E. Snow* had saddened the village of Blue Hill whence had come her captain and her crew. My grandfather, as has already been related, arrived in time to attend the services held for them, to be present, as it were, at his own funeral. There, in church, as he turned to face the choir, he saw my grandmother in the aforesaid poke bonnet with pink roses beneath the brim. Whether or not it was his first sight of her, I have forgotten, if, indeed, I ever knew. But certain it is that he saw her with clearer vision and with a quickening heart not often encouraged by the funerals of eighty years ago!

It was my grandfather himself who had been the messenger of such a cataclysmic disaster. From the castle of the Irish nobleman he had written to a Blue Hill shipmaster, one Captain John Closson, marking his letter "Per First Steamer for the United States." This letter, which I have in my possession, is too suggestive of the fruits of seafaring to be omitted. I give it here exactly as it is written, with no attempt to improve upon its spelling and its grammar, only inserting necessary capitalization and punctuation in which it is almost entirely lacking. Its terse, laconic phrasing, the unconscious irony of its understatement, its objectiveness throughout—these describe better than any words of my own, not so much my grandfather himself but rather the type of men to which he belonged—those who did "business in great waters" and who contributed most largely to the inestimable worth of a period in American life and history.

GALWAY, IRELAND, Feb. the 18eth, 1847.

Capt. Closson:

SIR:

It is with the deepest regret that I must inform you of the loss of the *Sarah E. Snow* and every soul on board except myself. We sailed from N. York Jan. the 3rd and on the 24eth when within 60 miles of the Irish coast while laying too in a heavy gale from the S. W. under a close reef maintopsail at 11 A.M. was struck by a heavy sea which knocked the vessel on her beam ends drowning the larbourd watch in the forecastle. The Capt. and myself being in the cabin at the time I succeded in getting out and got hold of a rope and saved myself. The Capt. got partly out, but the water rushing in washed him back twice. As soon as I got into the rigging, I threw down ropes in to the door and done all in my power to try to get him out, but it was impossible, the cabin doors being then all under water. I emediately cut the lanyards and the masts all went in the deck. In a few minuites she righted partly up, being then full of water, there being but two men left then, the rest having been swished of and drowned. We got on the quarter deck when she righted. The first sea that came over took of the second mate. The other man held on about half an hour and was washed of and I was left alone, there being no part of her out of water but the quarter deck and topgallant forecastle.

The gale continued verry heavy until the next day. The wind then abated a little. On the morning of the 27eth, I saw the land about 25 miles dist. the wind still continuing to the westward. At daylight on Thursday the 28eth I was then within four miles of the land, the wind blowing directly on with a verry heavy sea. At about 11 A.M. the people on shore saw me and came out from behind the island and took me of. The vessel, being then about 2 cables length from the breakers, when she struck the rock. The first sea turned her bottom up. I was carried on shore and kindly treated. Having had nothing to eat or drink all the time I was on the wreck I was scarcely able to walk. As soon as I was able, I got to the mainland and noted a protest and wrote to the consul to Galway who sent me money to get there. I shall leave here tomorrow for Liverpool and shall come to N. York in the first packet that sails. I should have wrote before, but there is no mail leaves England until the 1st of March.

There will be nothing of the vessel saved except the chains and anchors. I have sent the protest to Mr. Snow in Boston. The capt's body was not found. Two of the men in the forecastle was got and buried. I have got pretty well recovered now. I think I shall get to N. York about the first of April if nothing happens. Mr. Hause, the second mate, left in N. York, and my brother went in his place = [1] The vessel's freight out was insured in N. York for $4000. If there is anything you wish me to do about the insurance

[1] These two dashes are almost the only marks of punctuation in the original letter.

before I come home, right to me in N. York in the care
of Bret G. Vose.

I shall come direct home as soon as I get to N. York.

Yours with respect—

MELATIAH K. CHASE.

CHAPTER V

MY GRANDMOTHER'S HONEYMOON

FEW brides have had so eventful a honeymoon as my grandmother. This statement cannot, I feel sure, be termed sweeping even though it is curtailed neither by time nor by place.

She was married in the Congregational Church in Blue Hill on the 16th of July in the year 1849, two years and three months after my grandfather had fallen in love with her in the selfsame spot, but on a more sombre occasion. She was twenty-two years old, and my grandfather was twenty-six. She wore the first silk dress she had ever worn in all her life. It was of pearl grey taffeta striped in rose, made by her own hands in the modish, double skirt style with ample hoops and bishop's sleeves and with bows of rose velvet closing the basque and encircling the tiny waist. The neck and cuffs were finished with hemstitched ruffles in finest cambric. Although she secretly longed for one of the new, more stylish hats, which set well upon the head and featured not only broad streamers at the sides and rosettes above the ears, but a plume falling jauntily over the crown at the left, she acceded to my grandfather's sole request and wore a grey silk poke bonnet with a wreath of pink roses beneath the brim. She carried his gift, an ivory-handled pink silk parasol, which he had brought her from France and which attracted much attention by virtue of its convenient hinge, enabling one to adjust it at any angle against the sun.

In her spare hours from midwifery and seamstressing she had made her trousseau, allowing no fingers save her own to aid in its elaborate fashioning. Her underwear and night clothes were her especial pride. She had six of each article—six nightdresses and six frilled night-caps; six of every sort of petticoat then modestly worn; six pairs of drawers, their long legs trimmed with rows of fine tucks and edged with yards upon yards of Van Dyke crochet; six chemises. These last-named were formed with tiny cap sleeves, marvellously shirred and bordered with hemstitched ruffles. They were the pride of her entire outfit, having been made from sheer and expensive linen, for the purchase of which her parents had not been slow to criticize her. As children we were well-grounded in the details of my grandmother's trousseau. Indeed, to her dying day she never ceased to mourn its tragic loss, seemingly counting her own life but small compensation for those wondrously wrought chemises of fair (and expensive) linen floating through the blue-green depths of the South Atlantic.

My grandfather in July 1849 was the proud master and owner of a barque of fifteen hundred tons burden. He christened her *The Bride*. Chartered by a New York firm, she was to carry on her maiden voyage flour to Bermuda and, as a more precious freight, my grandmother, the one trunk which held all her wedding clothes, and the romantic hopes and plans of her and her husband. For this was to be no ordinary honeymoon. To my grandfather's travelled eyes Bermuda was just around the corner from Blue Hill. Picking up a mixed cargo there for England, they were to proceed across the Atlantic to Liverpool, thence to Cadiz, thence, after some weeks of Spanish life, through the Straits and across the Mediterranean and the Red Sea into the Indian Ocean toward Calcutta, thence up the Chinese coast to Shanghai. There they might linger, my grandfather spending some months in the coast-carrying trade, my grandmother remaining in the Shanghai home of some American merchants and seeing a bit of Oriental life. Then, if all things had gone well, they would continue their journeyings and their livelihood by proceeding across the Pacific laden with rice for California where the gold rush was on. And to terminate what was quite likely to be a two years' voyage with coast trading here and there, they would load up with gold ore and round the Horn for New York and home.

My grandmother, as she hemstitched the ruffles for her chemises, was probably quite unable to assimilate any of these forecastings. She had come from farming, not from seafaring stock; and Bangor, Maine, had been her *terminus ad quem*. But her personality at seventy was sufficiently intense and buoyant to suggest under what excitement she must have whipped and shirred at twenty.

They sailed from New York on the first day of August, 1849, after a fortnight of unparalleled adventurings. There was the purchase in a bewildering store of a brown fur muff and tippet, the former oblong and inclined to flatness, with dangling brown tassels at either end, the latter cut after the new Parisian shawl shape with pointed ends and rich satin clasps; there were introductions to obsequious and interested merchants, one of whom proferred a case of jellies and fruits to enliven the daily fare of *The Bride* by providing repasts more befitting a honeymoon; there was the startling and unforgettable taste of a delicacy quite unknown to her, ice cream, the sudden and unexpected coldness of which she never forgot; there was the exciting boarding of the ship, the acquaintance with her new and narrow quarters, the tidy, compact arrangement of her new possessions.

After four days at sea there occurred that colossal event, to which so many hours of my childhood were blissfully dedicated. Somewhere off Hatteras *The Bride* encountered a fearful gale. It rose suddenly without sufficient warning. At five one morning my grandmother was aroused in her berth by the appearance of my grandfather armed with a pair of his own woollen stockings and a sailor's peajacket and trousers. She would best get into these, he said, as he scented trouble. My grandmother told us how she was sitting filled with fear on the edge of her berth drawing on a woollen stocking when the ship capsized, how she completed her strange costuming at a stranger angle!

She was carried on the deck, now careening perilously above the engulfing waters, and lashed to a mast. There she remained for thirty-six black hours while the wind tore away the rigging and mountainous seas tore away her clothing. She told us of confusion unutterable, the screams of the sailors, the snapping and creaking of the ship, the cursing and the prayers. She told us of the frightful, suffocating impact of multitudinous waves, smiting the breath from her body, of intolerable suffering from hunger and cold and the more intolerable anguish, as the hours went on, from chafed and smarting flesh. We knew that the deafness which saddened sixty years of her life began with those monstrous seas as they washed over her head. Long before a British barque bore down upon them, fears of death had given place to ardent desire for it.

The British ship lay to in the semi-darkness, not daring to launch her boats even though the storm had abated. And then came that stupendous climax which in our minds always ranked our grandmother with those favoured ones of Scriptural record, with the daughter of Jairus, with Tabitha, and with Simon Peter's wife's mother. For according to her own asseveration she was saved by a miracle! A meteor fell, and by its light enabled the British captain to launch his boats and to take off the shipwrecked officers and crew.

As a child, I always saw this act of God as a gigantic ball of fire somewhat resembling my mother's wash-tub, suspended in mid-air above my grandfather's dismantled and ruined vessel; in fact, I was conscious of a bitter disappointment when, at a more mature age, I learned it was but a strange glow in the sky and over the waters. But my grandmother's telling of it, whatever impression she intended to convey, left nothing to be desired. Neither did her account of those events which followed hard upon their tardy saving. Stripped of all their earthly possessions, even to their clothing, they were taken on board the British ship which, fortunately for those days, carried a doctor. My grandmother was too ill to witness from her hospitable decks the final destruction of *The Bride*, which was swallowed by the sea in less than an hour after their rescue. But before they reached St. Georges, she was again ready to live.

I feel sure that her instinct for drama triumphed over even her complete and ruthless poverty as, helped by my grandfather and the British captain, she ascended the white steps of the leading St. Georges hotel. She was completely clad in sailor's clothing even to shoes. On the topmost step, to her dire, and, I dare to say, *delighted* embarrassment, one of her white woollen stockings escaped from its improvised garter and fell below the leg of her trousers. The news of her misfortune swept through the city, and she was almost immediately inundated with clothing of every description. Unfortunately, however, the Bermuda ladies were moved beyond the practical thought of consultation and comparison. For the first articles sent to minister to her necessities were a comical and lavish succession of thirteen white silk bonnets!

Within two months of the day of their wedding my grandparents were once more at home. But not for long. Insurance plus native resiliency procured another ship, the *Eliza Ann Chase*, in which they again set forth with yet another stock of wedding chemises. My grandmother, like many another woman of her generation who had chosen to marry a sailor, chose also to stay by him whatever the cost. Now fate changed her tactics and was kind. For twelve years my grandmother sailed, in comparative safety, only remaining at home during the months preceding the birth of her children. She read and sewed on the quarter deck in the sun of many foreign harbours; she lingered in foreign cities; she looked alike upon Moorish mosques and Gothic cathedrals; she tempered her Puritan inheritance with amiable and welcome leaven.

One cannot ask a better legacy than such a life affords, both to itself and to those who are reared upon its long effects. The breadth and depth of experience of my grandmother's seafaring years, grafted as they were upon a childhood and a youth of hardship and its attendant discipline, were bound to bear rich fruit. Nor was her lot unique in her generation or in her environment. It fell to other coast women of equally simple background and nurture and worked its gracious way with them also. It gave to their descendants more than can easily be estimated or measured. Maine in the heyday of sailing ships was yet a young State, separated only in 1820 from Massachusetts, its mother. By such fortunes as those of my grandmother she stamped her coast towns and villages with an indelible character, which is yet traceable, and thus established early her own personality.

In the great white houses of Searsport and Damariscotta, Belfast and Wiscasset, Bucksport and Blue Hill there still lingers something of that *venustas*, that *sales* and *urbanitas* extolled by Catullus—the enlightened heritage of those days when provincial minds met the larger, outer world across the seas. Such a possession will remain invincible armour against the new prosperity of the coast as long as such an inheritance is nurtured and cherished.

When I went to college in 1904, my grandmother, then nearing eighty, presented me, not without due formality, with one of the chemises of her second trousseau. Perhaps she gave it as a curious rather than as a useful article. I may say, however, that I wore it with pride, the hemstitched ruffles of its capped sleeves forming no insuperable obstacle to the swiss muslin evening gowns of twenty-five years ago!

PART IV

EDUCATIONAL IDEALS AND PRACTICES AT THE TURN OF THE CENTURY

CHAPTER I

EDUCATION AT HOME

(1)

THE sketch of my father already given has doubtless suggested that the education of his children was nurtured and developed at home quite as much as at school. In point of fact, home was unquestionably the larger factor of the two. Delightful as was the obsolete village school, which we attended for seven years and which taught us none too badly without any idea of "educational" precept, project, or experiment, we learned far more at home under the supervision and with the co-operation of our parents. My father was the instigator of various schemes for mental training and enrichment; he sowed the seed, as it were, likewise reaped the harvest and gazed upon his crop. It was my mother, however, who weeded and watered, harrowed and pruned, against the time of gathering into barns.

"Your father is likely to ask for the Roman Emperors any day. Put half an hour on them before you coast."

"Remember, your father wanted you to measure the wood-pile in cubic feet."

219

"Why not surprise your father by having your declension ready today instead of tomorrow?"

Such were the familiar injunctions that punctuated my childhood.

My mother taught me to read, or rather she conceived the plan by which I taught myself. In the early nineties, either in the school or in the home, there were no ingenious and "psychologically sound" methods of teaching a child to read. Phonetics was not employed nor was the recognition of words themselves without due regard to their component parts encouraged. Children learned their letters with the aid of blocks or of alphabetized and rhymed picture-books and in due course of time put the letters into words. In Blue Hill a kind of corporate pride and self-respect demanded that a child of four in the average well-regulated family should know the alphabet. When I had learned my letters, my mother utilized both my new knowledge and my passion for a pencil and paper by suggesting that I copy a small story-book word for word, crossing the *t*'s and dotting the *i*'s, combining the letters into their words by proper spacing, omitting no tiny, odd mark of punctuation. I have long since forgotten the name of the book over which I worked so many patient hours; but its first sentence remains with me after forty years: "It was Christmas eve in the little village of Marfield." I have forgotten, too, if indeed I ever knew, the steps by which it became evident to me that I was learning to read. Perhaps it did not *become* at all, but rather on a certain illumined day *was*, just as light in the story of the Creation did not come, but *was*.

It is recorded of that delightful and mighty eccentric, Thomas De Quincey, that he taught each of his many children at the age of two years to cut the pages of books without injury, thus inculcating in them a reverence for the printed word. New books in our home were not sufficiently plentiful for a family of our size to be instructed in this art. Nevertheless, we were early taught to handle books carefully and with deep respect. Any, or all, in our relatively small library was ours to examine; and the slightest mutilation was looked upon as a major offence.

When we were very young, my mother instituted a practice, the memory of which none of us would be without. During the winters, colder then than now, she was faced with the major problem of accomplishing her cooking and at the same time of keeping us secure from draughts in a none too well heated house. If she had us in the kitchen, the warmest room, we were constantly under foot; if she allowed us the run of the living-rooms, we were out of touch with her surveillance. During a particularly bitter January in my third or four year she conceived a novel and workable idea. My father at her suggestion and direction moved one morning from the library into the kitchen a certain old secretary, surmounted above its drawers with two shelves, the topmost flanked on either side with upright posts. To my father's amusement she placed on the top shelf her two oldest children, securing us with roller towels to the posts and at the same time binding to us the baby, who was placed in the middle. The logical entertainment for us in our exalted position was reading. My older sister, who read early and well, held in her lap our battered old *Grimm*, our *Andersen*, or *Robinson Crusoe* in one-syllabled words; and thus we spent many a morning for many a year even after the number on the top of the secretary increased. The winter sunlight lay on the yellow kitchen floor; the frost on the window-panes made a background of crystal fretwork for the red geraniums; the warm, heavy smell of ginger-snaps in the oven promised a mid-morning luncheon; my mother with a hint of flour on her pink cheek promised also as she sang that we should all "gather at the River." What wonder that in such surroundings certain books attained an eternal importance and clarity?

This custom was responsible also for banishing at least partially from our minds a strictly unpleasant connotation. From it roller-towels lost in a measure the significance with which in our family they were early invested. My mother, when we were scarcely out of our infancy, employed these with complete success as an aid in the punishment of sundry minor offences. A child who was needlessly peevish, selfish, or unwilling to co-operate in the larger interests of the family was liable to such correction, which was imposed in the following manner: The miscreant was swathed twice beneath his arms with a roller-towel and then hung to a convenient door-knob in such a way that his toes just touched the floor. The discomfort of this position was as nothing compared to the helpless ignominy which it both engendered and suggested. It was my mother's most salutary means of discipline, although my father's affirmation, that he came home one noon to find *four* doors thus encumbered, would seem to set at naught my assertion. Thus roller-towels from the beginning bred fear and suspicion within us—sentiments which my mother's more pleasant use of them on the old secretary did much to alleviate. In these overly-sanitary days when I perchance glimpse a rare roller-towel, I find myself, true to the psychologist, swept by two diametrically-opposed emotions!

When we grew older and entered school, my mother saw to it that the preparation of certain lessons at home was strictly carried out. She had no patience whatever with the claim we sometimes made that ample time was given us for such preparation in school. Such an idea, she affirmed, was a "crazy notion, worse than foolish." And if, after we had emerged from the insignificance with which her words always clothed us, we ventured to cite instances of excellent lessons prepared and recited at school, she entirely settled the matter by saying, "Quick in, quick out!" to which there was obviously no adequate response.

One hears a great deal today, especially in academic circles, about the difficulty of adjustment to four years of study. It is said with truth that young people entering college often do not know either how to concentrate upon their work or how to apportion their time. My mother's training was proof against any such mishaps in the later lives of *her* children. We learned early, in fact before we were six, to concentrate over our respective spelling-lessons, which were prepared immediately before bed-time and recited to my mother as she braided or curled or brushed our hair the next morning. As for the apportionment of our time, that was done likewise by her with accuracy and thoughtfulness.

Every evening except in summer, once the supper dishes had been cleared away and washed, our orderly and harmonious routine began. My father settled himself in his big chair in the library, an oracle who might be consulted in times of calamity or doubt. My mother procured her enormous mending-basket, heaped with underwear and stockings. As we grew older and entered the academy, the freight of this great basket was always weighted with books— her own Cæsar, Cicero, and Vergil. We always studied in the dining-room, each having his proper place around the lamp in the centre of the table and my mother sitting as at meal-times at the head. Even although the smaller children were required before their earlier bed-time to put but fifteen minutes upon their spelling or sums, my mother insisted that they sit with the group for that space of time. Half-sized ones of grammar-school age wrestled in comparative silence with abstruse problems concerning the cube root of monstrous numbers; or the manual talents of Mr. A., Mr. B., and Mr. C.; or the ways, means, and price of papering a room with many annoying windows of differing sizes. My father in the library adjoining was usually too much engrossed in his book or too tired to throw much light on such practical matters, although he was always glad to explain the Monroe Doctrine or the Alien and Sedition Acts.

My mother, who was never balked by the most intricate and mysterious alliances of Messrs. A., B., and C., was, however, happiest and most at home when, once in the academy, my sisters and I embarked upon our Latin. The Greek she left to my father. She spread her books before her, placing the mending-basket to one side; and as she darned the frayed heels of numerous stockings or inserted ingenious patches in our winter underwear, she kept her eyes sufficiently well upon the passage in question to assist or, as frequently happened, to admonish us. When we had once begun translation in earnest with the *Gallic Wars*, she was unsparing in her criticism of our clumsy construings, our laborious English renderings. Once we had mastered an assignment literally, she insisted that we go over and over it until the English was simple and accurate, less Latinized in sound and aspect. She was, in point of fact, an unrelenting taskmaster.

"Orgetorix," said my mother, holding a pair of

worn red flannel drawers to the light, "would turn over in his grave could he hear your translation!"

She was quite as relentless in her supervision of the beginner whose task weighed more and more heavily as the first and second declensions and conjugations gave place to ablative absolutes and the intricacies of clauses contrary to fact. How we laboured evening by evening over the Latin equivalents of those stately incidents of Roman society, those slow tragedies, those matters of ancient conduct and ethics!

My uncle gave the beautiful red roses in his garden to the son-in-law of his friend, the eloquent lawyer.

I have frequently told your brother not to treat his noble father with disrespect.

What was the reason that your virtuous stepmother hanged herself?

Things being thus, I have been obliged to abandon my journey to the villa of Anthony, my grandmother's bailiff.

The noble Epaminondas asked whether his shield were safe.

If your neighbour were to have a better horse than yours is, would you prefer your horse or his?

When I began my study of Greek in my second year at the village academy, my father became my preceptor at home. In the matter of accents and breathings he gave no quarter, being as ruthless as one of the Homeric gods. Declensions and conjugations must be accurately memorized, recited, and written; and he would admit no insuperable difficulties even when I arrived at the verbs in μι. Once I had reached the easier and more thrilling labours of translation, we held together for two years high and delighted converse with the mighty dead. It is but fair to record, however, that he worried not a little over my "new rendering" of the ει sound. He had always used the ī, and he heartily disliked the ā. If he had had a trying case in court, or if rheumatism, ever the stubborn tenant of his earthly tabernacle, was annoying him, he was likely to deliver a tirade against this innovation while I sat embarrassed, feeling upon my shoulders the full weight of the bad taste and worse scholarship of the modern Greek grammarians. But my father never suggested that I depart from the pronunciation I was learning at school nor did he attempt to change the mind of my Greek teacher. Disappointed though he was, he was quick to recognize authority and was perforce content with instructing me how it used to be done and how it might well have been continued.

(2)

Some of my readers may object to my suggestion that such evenings as ours with our lessons were *typical* of any period or of any environment. If they do so object, it is because, in the first place, they do not know the integrity and the solidarity existing from generation to generation in a rural American community, English by race and tradition; and be-

cause, in the second place, they have not recognized
the synthesis, still operative in the nineteenth century, between the primitive American setting and the
intellectual heritage of the country.[1] Not for nothing
were more than three hundred leaders of the 1630
Puritan migration Cambridge and Oxford men!
They placed a stamp upon New England, which
New England carried in the eighteenth and nineteenth centuries to the Middle and Far West,—a
mark of the union, the blending, even the fusion of
the manual and the intellectual, of the nurture of a
cultivated tradition along with the necessary nurture
of fields and of families. For more than two centuries
English Americans recognized with no sense of dis-
parity the perennial nobleness and sacredness of hard,
unremitting toil existing side by side with the perennial nobleness and sacredness of the things of the
mind. Probably no other country can quietly boast of
just such an exalted synthesis.

In the mid-nineteenth century a caller at the home
of Sarah Alden Ripley found her employed in four
seemingly divergent tasks: She was rocking the
baby's cradle; she was shelling peas; she was teaching Calculus to one Harvard student; she was cor-
recting a translation of Sophocles made by another
Harvard student. In the late nineteenth century my
mother, patching a pair of red flannel drawers and at
the same time insisting that Orgetorix, chief of the

[1] For a most interesting presentation of this very matter see O. W.
Firkins, *Undepicted America*, in *The Yale Review*, Autumn, 1930.

Helvetians, should receive his just due in a decent
and decorous English translation, presents an interesting and accurate parallel. Granting that my parents may have been unusual in their classical training,
may have been more assiduous than some in the intellectual discipline of their children, I still maintain
that they were in no sense unique. Hundreds of other
Maine families in the nineties in communities still
English, yet unhampered by English social traditions
through their American heritage, believed and be-
haved in precisely the same manner. If their children
did not study Latin around a common table (and
many of them did) they studied history and geometry. The fact is that they *studied* with a naturalness
and a faith unknown to the rank and file of twentieth
century America. For twentieth century America has
not in any such degree that originality of synthesis
which was still her inestimable possession in the nineteenth century. Her doors have been further opened;
she has become assimilative, comprehensive, diversi-
fied; the influences upon her are now European
rather than those brought by herself from England
to be made at once her own and built into the very
fabric of her fresh and peculiar identity. Such new
influences and assimilations, together with the swift
passing of the necessity for manual labour, may prove
altogether desirable. Who can yet say? I mention
them, not to develop a thesis, but to point a fact—
the fact that they have caused or at least are causing
the vanishing of that native American distinction and

stamp, that aristocratic fellowship of the hand and the mind. But that America once saw no dissimilarity between a milking-stool and a love of Shakespeare, between a plough and the thoughts above Tintern Abbey, between the *Gallic Wars* and a pair of red flannel drawers—this remains her glory and the pride of us who were nourished in a waning yet still potent tradition.

(3)

Our education at home was by no means relegated to our books or to the practices and pastimes derived therefrom. Not a little of it arose from the performance of our daily chores. More of it came from the fact that we were trained early to be intelligently alert to the countryside about us. Although we were not farmers, we, like most other village families, cultivated a goodly portion of our few acres. The knowledge of the difference between a radish and a turnip, an onion and a beet, was seemingly born with us, so soon was it made manifest. We followed the plough in the spring and watched the shaping of the none too fertile soil into garden rows. We helped in weeding and hoeing; we picked potato bugs and dropped them willingly into tin cans; we trained beans and peas to become acquainted with poles and brush for climbing.

My father taught us to recognize familiar trees and even to distinguish between the various maples, oaks, and pines. A lover of birds himself, he told us all that he knew about them. I especially fell, perhaps more than the other children, under his guidance in this direction; for in his later years, not being overly well, he took long, quiet walks in the early morning and encouraged my company. We went before breakfast in the spring, swinging our walking-sticks as we breasted the long hill which led us into open roads or perchance into wood-paths. With him I heard near at hand the drumming of a partridge; with him I discovered my first oven-bird's nest and marvelled at its intricacy; with him I rested on a stump while we turned excitedly the pages of my small bird-guide to make sure that the sparrow in question was actually a grasshopper sparrow and not just a smaller member of the same family with a throat affliction of some sort.

But perhaps the greatest influence upon us in matters as wide and beneficent as these was exerted by an old gardener, David Emerson by name, whom we in common with certain other families employed for certain days in the spring, summer, and fall. For twenty years his was a familiar figure; and although he has now passed to his celestial cultivating of those "sweet and pleasant flowers" in greener and goodlier walks than ours, I still see him bending over our garden borders and commenting sceptically upon such new importations as salpiglossis and mourning-brides.

He was always, indeed, sceptical of innovation of every sort. He wanted the same flowers in the same places each year. If, after hours spent in conning seed catalogues on stormy February afternoons, we decided as a family upon such a radical change as a substitution of marigolds for nasturtiums in a given spot, we knew we had David to reckon with. He was even more intractable when it came to experimenting with a new species. I did not understand then as I do now that the reason for his stubbornness was his dislike of subjecting Maine coast soil to the bringing up of a stranger. He had a loyalty to the earth, the soil, the brown, clay-streaked glacial drift of Maine, which was almost terrible in its intensity. He could not bear to admit its failure when heliotrope was but pindling and when some new lilies failed to appear at all. Far rather, with fierce protection, would he lay the blame upon his own shoulders. When he turned up huge, steaming clods of loam in the spring with his spade, he always broke and crumbled them with his feet or his great, red hands instead of with his hoe. Like Gawain or Antæus or others of the fabled ones, he seemed to derive his strength from the Earth, his Mother; and in return he became her partner and support. Sufficiently urged or finally commanded, he *would* plant new and strange seeds or seedlings; but he always held them in his hands with suspicion and he always saw to it that the soil was freed from any responsibility by saying over and over again, "It's no likely plant for us down here."

His hatred and distrust of innovation extended perhaps even to his clothes, for year after year he wore a work-suit of denim in ugly brown and yellow checks. Caked with soil and torn in a dozen places, it yet reappeared April by April. For years the selfsame three-cornered rent remained just below one shoulder; and I remember as a child explaining to myself that it could not be mended or patched on the Scriptural grounds of the inadvisability of putting new cloth into old garments!

He was a great, burly man of tremendous physical strength. He was getting old while I was still young; and his head was bald above a grizzled reddish beard. He walked with a heavy tread, plodding yet strangely rhythmic, as though his ally, the soil, lent him with each step a slow yet even spring. He came at six in the morning in the spring and summer, having walked the two miles from his home in more isolated country; he worked until nightfall. We paid him one dollar a day; and my mother always had the bill ready for him to fold away carefully in an inside pocket safer than those of his work-suit.

My mother found in him an invaluable assistant. Not only did he keep our grounds and our flower beds in excellent condition, but he also kept her younger children in excellent behaviour. Constrained and taciturn as was his outward bearing and manner, a kinder person never breathed. We, and in their turn our younger brothers and sisters, followed him for hours on end as he went about his work, removing and replacing the banking-boards and brush, raking the dry fall leaves or the wet spring ones, preparing his cherished soil for winter or for spring. Or we stood transfixed while he thinned out or transplanted seedlings, so tiny that it seemed they must be injured by the slightest pressure of his great fingers. He did not talk much with us of his own accord; yet he was never slow to answer our questions, and I have gained from him not only a passion for gardening but practically all the knowledge I have ever had concerning that bountiful pursuit.

As season followed season and he and we grew older, we began to be aware of certain traits in him, to look upon them and to know their goodness. He had a passion for order. He could not tolerate a misplaced tool, or a geranium out of line, or a given piece of work left half complete. He loved his work with a devotion evident in his very stooping above a garden bed; and when seventy crept upon him and Maine coast rheumatism began its tenacious hold, insisting that he kneel no more upon the damp ground, his zeal and eagerness somehow passed down the long handle of his hoe into the waiting earth.

For he and the soil enjoyed a kinship not often felt to such a degree, and his intense jealousy of its very inadequacy grew upon him with the passing of time. Once when in the early twenties I returned from the Middle West after three years among the fertile black fields of Wisconsin, I favoured him with a discourse on the rockless, clayless loam of that rich state. There, I said, one did not need to labour early and late to ensure success; there roses were not so prone to winter-killing or sweet peas such an easy prey to green aphis and red spiders; there corn and wheat stretched for miles, unbroken by gullies or by patches of sandy gravel. While I talked, he stood leaning upon his hoe near some small lilacs which he had been clearing of witch-grass, that mulish product of Maine coast soil. Somewhat discomfited by his profound silence, for he answered not a word nor vouchsafed me even so much as a glance, I continued with the agricultural pre-eminence of the state of California which I had recently visited. Calla lilies there, I said, were mowed down with a scythe like hay; geraniums there grew to veritable trees, decorating even the chimneys with their blossoms; heliotrope there bore not the slightest resemblance to those frail flowers which he had striven in vain to nurture in our garden beds.

One should not go about breaking old hearts, even in the self-sufficiency of the early twenties. But David's restraint was equal to the occasion. If he questioned my loyalty to the soil of my native state, from which he and I had come and to which we should go, he was too much of a gentleman to give expression to his disappointment. When I had at last done, he only plunged his hoe deeper into the roots of the witch-grass.

"What I'm figurin' on," he said, "is the gardener. He must be a mighty onimportant person out in them states!"

CHAPTER II

OUR EARLY VENERATION OF AUTHORS

(1)

MY father was possessed of an old custom, the source of which was a mystery and the observance of which, as we grew older, caused us no little embarrassment. Once our tardy Maine spring had actually come, he began his curious indulgence and continued therein until October. At noon he emerged from his office and walked homeward in his sedate fashion, up the village street, *carrying his collar and tie in his left hand.* The rare extremes of heat on the Maine coast could not explain his habit, for it was in no sense dependent upon the weather. Our respect for him forbade any questioning and demanded likewise that we stifle any mortification when, as sometimes happened in the summers, strangers greeted him in this strange undress. My mother, though often approached by us on the matter, could afford no solution. Perhaps it must be accepted as an interesting commentary on the relative simplicity of a by-gone age, for surely no one in his senses in this sophisticated era would enter lightly upon such extraordinary behaviour! The few occasions, therefore, when he abandoned his practice stand out clearly in my mind. I learned early, in fact, that any deviation therefrom was a sign of extreme agitation on his part. If things were as they should be, he carried his collar and tie; if things were otherwise, he wore them.

One such rare occasion occurred early in the month of September in the year 1892. I was at that time approaching the age of six, and every detail of that noon-day hour is indelibly impressed upon my mind. In his left hand, as he came up the street, my father carried, instead of his collar and tie, the Boston *Herald*; and his face as he entered the driveway through the white gate confirmed my suspicion that something was fundamentally wrong. We were not left long in suspense.

"John Greenleaf Whittier," said my father to my mother at the kitchen stove, "is dead." He repeated his information in a louder tone to my grandmother by the dining-room window, whose face immediately registered surprise and sorrow.

It was in a subdued atmosphere that we sat down to dinner. Young as were my sister Mildred and I at eight and six, we knew John Greenleaf Whittier. From the game of Authors we knew his bald head and bearded face; from my mother's reading to us we knew *Snowbound* and *The Swan Song of Parson Avery*. But above all we knew that he was a poet; and even at our ages we held poets, indeed all writers of books, in veneration. We knew them as a race of men and women set apart from us ordinary folks. We knew them as immortals who engrossed my father's time and attention, who provided us with material for manifold feats of memory, who made delightful our evening reading hour. During dinner my father read to us all the newspaper account of Whittier's death and supplemented it with timely remarks of his own concerning the poet's labours in the interest of freedom for the slaves. It was borne in upon us that a good and great man, as well as a famous poet, had passed; and that afternoon we made no remonstrance when my mother suggested that the three oldest of us learn each an appropriate stanza from his poems to recite to my father before bedtime. On the following Sunday when the minister from the pulpit read one of Whittier's hymns, and included in his long prayer our corporate thanks to God for such a splendid life, we felt a pleasant sense of comparative acquaintance with nobility and fame.

Two years later our household was again shaken by another untoward event. This was in December 1894. The season being inclement, my father's collar and tie must have remained in their rightful positions, for I do not recall any outward and visible sign of his excitement, saddened though he was. Indeed, it was my grandmother who felt most keenly the death of Robert Louis Stevenson and who communicated to us her own distress. She was an avid reader of *Treasure Island, Kidnapped* and *David Balfour;* and she had also, as was meet with her dramatic nature, long cherished a deep interest in the details of Stevenson's spectacular life,—his illness in America, his sojourn under such theatrical circumstances in Samoa. His early death filled her heart with sorrow and her vivid mind with potentialities for conversations with her neighbours. I remember these colloquies which took place over the driveway gate or in our living-room; I recall my grandmother's sombre and yet thrilling recital of every detail. Thus, the Road to Tusitala and the burial upon the Samoan hill summit, as well as the almost abject devotion to Stevenson felt by so many thousands of persons even in remote places, were graven upon my consciousness long before editions and biographies crowded the library shelves of many a country.

As a village we took a special interest and pride in the Longfellows, both the poet and his brother, Samuel, the writer of hymns. The latter, indeed, many years before my birth had spent several summers among us, and stories of his benevolence as well as of his solitary, reflective habits were still current. Naturally we children, reared on *Hiawatha* and *Evangeline*, chose the greater to the lesser light. The poet himself, in the early fifties, had spent certain summer months in one of the old houses near the bay; in fact, he had written not a few of his later poems therein under the obvious inspiration not only of the Mount Desert Hills but of Blue Hill Mountain itself. When at ten and twelve we were engaged at school or at home in sentimental perusal of the deathbed of Gabriel or of Evangeline's walk to church with her curious "chaplet of beads and her missal," we used to gaze upon the windows of the house which had sheltered him and were indignant that no one seemed now to know just which room had been his own.

In the matter of Longfellow our family, indeed, enjoyed a major distinction which we children were not slow to seize upon and work to its limit. Our grandfather, our mother's father, when a boy had once met the poet upon the beach. My mother told us that Mr. Longfellow was engrossed at that exciting moment in the contemplation of a sea urchin, an ordinary star-fish, and that our grandfather himself had actually been drawn into the holy of holies by having put to him by the poet a question concerning the nature of the creature.

"What do you know about a star-fish?" the poet had actually asked of our grandfather, a Blue Hill boy on a Blue Hill beach.

The possession of this question would in itself have been sufficient to ensure our prestige, to suggest that one close to us had enjoyed an enviable intimacy with him who in the nineties was still the Poet of poets. But in point of fact the question had been followed by a breath-taking assertion to my grandfather on the part of Mr. Longfellow, which added immeasurably to our family renown. Without waiting for a reply he had remarked quite of his own free will,

"Boys always know everything!"

We could never be adequately grateful to our

grandfather for this anecdote even although, from its sudden cessation, he seemed to have forgotten any rejoinder he may have made. Him we knew little because of his early removal and residence away from Blue Hill; but we were perennially glad of this incomparable experience which he had enjoyed and which among our associates surrounded us with such an halo.

(2)

At the age of eleven I was able to supplement the laurels thus afforded through a member of my immediate family by certain of my very own. For in the winter of the year 1898 I met my first author! This momentous occasion was given to me as a birthday present by my father and constituted then as now one of the high-water marks of my life.

The author was Laura E. Richards. Among the living, modern writers of my childhood she was almost without a peer. Her one rival in the composition of books primarily for children was, of course, Kate Douglas Wiggin; and our pride in the fact that both were Maine women was intense. We used to quarrel for hours over the relative merit and appeal of *Captain January* and *Timothy's Quest*, of *Three Margarets* and *A Summer in a Canyon*. But after I had actually seen Mrs. Richards in the flesh, had really sat on a hassock at her feet, had listened to her own voice as she read of old Captain January's finding of Star Bright, and had—incredible as it might seem!—been singled out by her for definite, direct and soul-shaking address—after these things had come to pass and been believed by my covetous friends, even *The Birds' Christmas Carol* was relegated, for a time, to a somewhat paltry position.

It was, as I have said, in the winter of 1898 that the adored and famous author of *Captain January* came to the neighbouring city of Ellsworth to speak and to read in one of the churches there. The month was February. I was to accompany my father, who was due to hold court in Ellsworth; and I was to be taken to the evening address by a friend of my mother's. The weather was very cold and the snow unusually deep. I remember my mother's misgivings concerning the wisdom of my venture on the fourteen-mile journey and my own sickening fears lest at the eleventh hour I should be ruthlessly snatched from my first glimpse of fame. But it was finally concluded that I should go, with folded newspapers across my chest beneath my heavy coat, with a soap stone at my feet, and a hot baked potato in either mittened hand. At the half way village of Surry, where we planned to arrive about the time the noon potatoes should be done in Surry ovens, we would replenish our supply.

I was grateful to my father for not talking much on the long, cold drive, for I wanted to enjoy to the full the thrills of anticipation. From time to time I said over to myself bits of *Captain January* which I knew by heart, wondering meanwhile how they would sound from the mouth of their creator; for the weekly county paper had expressly stated that the noted author would read "at some length from her most famous volume." When we at last reached Ellsworth in the early afternoon and the friend in question exclaimed over the tip of my nose, which she declared was frostbitten, I was so steeped in my dreams as to feel only irritation at her kindness and concern.

That evening I sat on the very doorsill of complete enchantment. I can never forget one moment of it. Today authors are so many and so common that even high school youngsters treat them with friendly nonchalance. But in the nineties this was not so. Then they pursued a profession, or better still a "calling," not a mere trade. Then their thinner ranks were not threatened by hundreds dangerously infected with *cacoethes scribendi* and confident of immediate success. Then the peculiar power which they possessed (or which one *believed* they possessed) was not advertised as easily attainable through a six-weeks' correspondence course. Instead, they dwelt apart in a rarefied atmosphere compounded of charm, insight, and genius; and I, sitting at eleven in the front seat of the First Congregational Church of Ellsworth, in my best dress of blue serge, with a large bow of white china silk beneath my chin, asked only to gaze upon greatness with humility and adoration.

The author of *Captain January* wore a dress of

black velvet, with silver-buckled shoes upon her feet and around her bare white neck a string of pearls which she handled as she talked. She was rather a large woman with white hair and a mobile, vivacious face. So rapturous was my contemplation of her every feature and of every detail of her costume, and so forceful was my stamping of each upon my mind that much of what she said must have later escaped my memory, intently as I listened at the time. I do recall her courteous reminder that we were not strangers to her, but instead her friends by the very fact that we read and loved her books; but the rest has slipped away perhaps because it was so eclipsed by her subsequent behaviour.

When she had finished her address proper, she prepared to read to us. For this purpose she descended the pulpit steps and sat on the floor level in a huge red velvet chair by a small table that held a lamp and a glass of water. I had been so staring at her with big, round eyes, which scarcely blinked for fear of missing her slightest movement, that I suppose her own eyes were irresistibly drawn to me sitting just before her in my blue dress and big white tie. There can, indeed, be no other explanation of her notice, for I was distinctly a plain child with nothing whatever to make me stand out save very red cheeks, which that night, I presume, were redder than ever. But be that as it may, explain it as you will, the incredible fact is, was, and will always be that she beckoned to *me* to draw near her in her great red chair. Astonishment and incredulity almost held me to my seat had not the practical sense of my guardian brought me to my senses and demanded that I move quickly forward to the threshold of genius.

"I always did like red-cheeked girls," she said, as she took my hand in hers. "And now won't you sit by me on this footstool while I read?"

Other children then were invited and came, bringing with them crickets and hassocks from the various pews. But for them the invitation was general; none was singled out as I had been. I do not remember her reading, her rendering of my favourite passages, much as I had planned to do so. The overwhelming fact that I was sitting at her feet, so near that her black velvet dress was shimmering against my fingers, that she had asked my name and was calling me by it—this was sufficient to blind me even to the tears in *Captain January*.

I could not speak a word as my mother's friend took me home with her for the night, as I brushed my teeth in silence, got into my flannel nightgown, and mumbled embarrassed prayers in incoherent whispers. She must have thought me a stodgy child, indeed. Nor could I say much even to my father on our homeward drive the next day through the continued cold and snow. My voice returned, however, when I related over and over to my sisters and my friends every detail of the evening, dwelling minutely on my own preferment, my elevation to the highest seat. Also I swung for some months the balance in favour of my adored one and against her honoured rival. Yet there was an intangible something which I did not tell, which I could not have told if I would—an inviolable sense of Experience within experience and transcending the fruits thereof.

CHAPTER III

THE VILLAGE SCHOOL

ACCORDING to all modern standards, I was very badly educated, if educated at all, in the village school of Blue Hill. This institution in the nineties was almost wholly didactic, allowing the will comparatively little freedom and lending no encouragement whatsoever to individual quirks and idiosyncrasies. The "self" and its "expression" were entirely (perhaps wholesomely) neglected in the schoolroom; on the playground it found then, as always, various ways and means of asserting itself. Our rigid, unyielding days were governed by precept upon precept, line upon line; our preferences in any matter were rarely, if ever, consulted. From nine o'clock in the morning until four o'clock in the afternoon we did precisely as we were told to do. That the occasional revolutionary among us was rarely upheld by public opinion and that the vast majority of us loved school, with all its relentlessness, would seem to bear evidence that our training was neither wholly fallacious nor absurd.

At least we were never looked upon as "cases," psychological or pathological; and if we were too early compelled to adjust ourselves to the larger whole, we were but learning one of the inexorable laws of human existence, which, so far as the cursory observer can gather, is not run on the principle of doing precisely as one pleases. After all, I am inclined to think that on the whole we fared rather fortunately. And certainly the sources for humour which those years afforded cannot be lightly set aside upon any balance sheet of the assets and the liabilities for life and living.

The school-house, then as now, stood upon a hill overlooking the village and the sea. Although it was neither "red" nor "little," it was an old building. The parents of all the occupants of my day and generation had been trained within its doors. Ugly and ungainly in its high, rectangular architecture, the sternness of its aspect without was quite in harmony with the rules it enforced within. It held two large rooms, the downstairs, or lower school, ministering to children up to ten years, the upstairs, or grammar school, attending to the needs of those from ten to thirteen or fourteen. Grades were unknown, although classes were recognized and named by letters. Each room was taught by a harassed and over-worked woman, who with upwards of twenty recitations a day in the essentials, had no time to attend to the frills and extras even although she had known anything about them or discerned any value therein.

The furnishings of the two rooms bore sturdy witness, not only to municipal poverty, but also to a strict regard for essentials only. With the five or six straight rows of double seats extending from the airtight stove in the rear to the teacher's platform, the long, hard settees for recitations before and below the teacher's desk, a globe, half a dozen somewhat obsolete maps, there was absolutely nothing to charm or to waylay. Between the two large blackboards, which formed the front wall of both the lower and the upper room, hung a picture, its subject, in each case, stirring to the senses but likely to pall upon one after years of constant gazing. Moses had been the artist's model. Downstairs, he lay in the bulrushes with Pharaoh's daughter peeping at him in somewhat wild surmise; upstairs, in a thunder storm with a terrifying display of lightning he was prepared on Mount Sinai to receive the Ten Commandments, which in two tablets of stone could be seen hurtling from the heavens in his general direction. This portrayal was not a little nervously upsetting to the child just promoted to the upper school, not only because of its predominant position which demanded one's attention, but also because of the prayerful attitude of Moses which suggested his unawareness of the feat about to be required of him. I remember many worried moments of my own lest he should prove incompetent.

These studies in Moses were the only ornaments of the rooms unless, indeed, the sententious declarations above the respective blackboards could be termed ornaments. In the lower school the little girls on the right were faced daily with the following weighty charge in large black letters against a white ground:

I shall pass through this world but once. Therefore, any good deed which I can do or any kindness which I can show to any fellow being, let me do it NOW. *Let me not defer or neglect it, for I shall not pass this way again.*

On the left side the little boys were doubtlessly well warned by the Apostle James:

The tongue is a little member, but boasteth great things. Behold how great a matter a little fire kindleth!

In the upper school the admonitions did not lessen in their intensity. For the girls, still on the right:

Labour to keep alive in thy breast that little spark of celestial fire called Conscience.

For the boys:

Seest thou a man diligent in his business? He shall stand before kings; he shall not stand before mean men.

So far as I can remember these maxims did not change during my seven years of residence; indeed, the very fact that they are so imperishably stamped upon my mind would seem sufficient proof of their tenure. They, and Moses, received inevitable attention whenever one's eyes were raised from book or slate, especially since the small-paned windows in either room were placed so judiciously high in the walls that anyone desiring to look upon hills and sea could do so only at the peril of breaking the rule in regard to position.

Our teachers changed as seldom as the maxims which they were supposed to emulate as well as to enforce. They were usually home products, trained, if trained at all, at a neighbouring normal school. Precise and inflexible as was their instruction, which deviated little from the printed page, obsolete and probably unsound as were their methods, they yet performed their task with the oneness of mind extolled and practised by Saint Paul. They commanded respect toward themselves; they demanded concentration on a given lesson, and they got it. Whether the means they employed were good or ill, at least the end justified them. We learned to sit still and study even though the assignment in question could be satisfactorily discharged by a literal repeating of lines and paragraphs.

They inspired, too, or at least developed, an intense pride in learning and learning well. To fail to "hand in" one's examples, to miss a word in spelling, to be unable to locate Puget Sound or to bound Idaho when such knowledge had been required—these things were held by tacit consent to be deplorable lapses, compensated for only by fresh resolves and seemly tears. To be kept after school was occasion for lowered eyes and flushed cheeks when one's classmates filed out to the tune of *John Brown's Body* or *Marching Through Georgia*, led by the teacher and sung by all in good standing. Today I look in vain

among schools and colleges for such solidarity of outlook, such strength of public opinion. In my seven
years at the village school I missed but two words in
spelling, and I cite no remarkable record. The first
word was *cousin*, missed on the day when a new sister
made her surprising advent; the second was *exile*,
missed also following the arrival one noon of my
second brother. Although these disasters were in part
explainable by untoward circumstances, nevertheless
the remedy for them remained the same, and I
copied each upon my slate fifty times before my confused and contrite release. The city of Vienna even
yet connotes to me neither cultured society, nor tim-
bered houses, nor musical festivals. I know it chiefly
on account of its exports recorded in the eighties by
our geography. For on one memorable day I failed
to recite when bidden, "The exports of Vienna are
sugar beets, grain, and lumber," and must needs remain after school to copy one hundred times upon
the blackboard the sentence I had thus offended.

Our teachers, in the nineties, were held to be at
their noblest and best when they supplemented or
complemented the ministers in religious and ethi-
cal instruction. No problems of sectarianism disturbed the rigid conduct of our morning devotions at
school. The Bible was read to us, and we recited
verses or, as often happened, complete Psalms therefrom. My teacher in the upper school for three years
employed the original though rather confusing custom of prayer in behalf of individual shortcomings.

I remember one ironic petition in my own behalf. I was observed in the act of administering a shaking, accompanied by slaps, to an associate; and God was summarily enjoined before the whole school to be merciful unto me, an obvious sinner of an especially deep dye. But the teacher had not seen and to this day does not know that the expression of my righteous anger had as its cause the slow dismembering of a fly caught upon a window pane and compelled, by the recipient of my blows and shakes, to lose its legs one by one.

In the lower school the morning religious instruction and exercise were followed by the recital of what we called "Manners." We even used the word in its singular form: The aphorism or injunction for which each was responsible we termed a "manner." For the searching out and the composition of his daily "manner" each child was a law unto himself; perhaps, indeed, it was the one part of the day's inflexible programme which can be called entirely self-directing. We culled these "manners" from books, from parents, from memory, or in cases of the eleventh hour from our own heads; there was no rule against reasonable repetition provided the same child did not too frequently recite the same "manner" or that the same "manner" were not proffered twice on the same morning by two different children.

The philosopher Epictetus, who objected to the laying down of rules, particularly rules of etiquette, would have been sadly annoyed at the enjoyment we derived and the glibness we displayed in this peculiar exercise. As the teacher called the roll, each child rose, stood by his seat in the prescribed position, and delivered himself of his "manner." Even the littlest were not excused. The subjects of the "manners" varied from the high affairs of ethics to the more practical concerns of decent and decorous living. A few examples will suffice to suggest their limitless scope and range. A serious, frail little girl, whose general make-up denied an ounce of drama, was given to crying out in impassioned tones, "In case of shipwreck, save the women and children first!" A fat little boy in very tight trousers, who has since become one of the financial props of Boston, furnished proof for the once popular contention concerning the New England morning meal by his reminder, repeated as often as possible and always with a suggestion of regret: "Never ask for two pieces of pie at breakfast." The most popular "manner" of a drab, prosy child, who usually remained for weeks on end at the foot of the spelling-class, echoed her mother's widespread talents as a housewife: "In sweeping a room, never forget the corners."

Our text-books in the village school changed quite as seldom as maxims, manners, or teachers. They were supplied us by the town funds, never in too flourishing a state, and so long as they held together, it was thought neither wise nor necessary to supersede them with newer, more up-to-date volumes. If our geography continued to call a piece of western land a territory long after it had become a state, or lacked the division of Dakota into North and South, we remained ignorant of these milestones in progress unless our teacher or our parents came to the rescue. If our history concluded its pages, as ours did, with the administration of Rutherford B. Hayes, our teacher was usually able to supply anything of importance which had occurred thereafter.

This unwillingness, or inability, to make frequent changes in text-books worked out particularly happily, for us at least, in the matter of Readers. So far as I can remember I used the same Reader over a period of many beneficial years. Since reading was the only study in which I was proficient, I was promoted early to the most advanced book and continued blissfully therein until I knew it from cover to cover. Mr. Mark Sullivan, in his interesting and valuable work, *The Turn of the Century*, gives unlimited credit to the McGuffey Readers. According to him, the inspiration which gave birth to American statesmen, clergymen and teachers in the 19th century, should be generously laid at the feet of William McGuffey. Personally I cannot accord him the most humble palm. His work was unknown to us, although he may well have contributed to the making of my parents. The Reader upon which I was reared was compiled gloriously by a man named Mr. Harvey. Since it was the fifth in a series, there were presumably four others to his credit although I never knew them. Presumably the fare set before me in this book was far beyond my powers of digestion; nevertheless, I tasted, sampled, and devoured everything that there was from the *Inchcape Rock* and *Lord Ullin's Daughter* to *Thanatopsis, Washington's Inaugural Address,* and Shakespeare's Trial Scene. It is difficult to understand, or to state, just how such an advanced and dignified volume ministered to very young children. Surely most of its selections were far beyond our comprehension, even though sanguine minds attribute to us in largest measure the mystical powers held to be ours by the poet. Nevertheless, the prescribed reading and memorizing of the prose and verse therein constituted one of the inestimable gifts of the village school. We became familiar with words not in our common speech, with the rise and fall of measured cadences, with the sonorous rhythms of English prose at its best. And although I have never seen Mr. Harvey's Reader from those days to this, I count its long-continued use as one of my greatest blessings, and thank the school which harboured it in days when food for children was fast becoming predigested and, without doubt, far more reasonable.

Neither space nor the indulgence of readers permits the recording of those incidents and customs which made life in the village school such a dramatic one in spite of the strict division of our hours, the orderly precision of one task after another. At the beginning of the term there was always the early rising, the swift performance of one's chores in order

that one's coveted seat might be secured, the possible
appearance of oneself in a new dress, the exhibiting
to one's friends of new pencil-boxes, tablets, and
slates. There was always the possibility of a new sign
manual conceived by a practical teacher, and announced on the first day of school—the index finger
of the raised hand signifying one urgent request, two
fingers another, three yet a third. There was the infrequent chance that a prize might be offered *for the
best map of the United States* or *for a perfect record
in attendance or in spelling.* And if all else failed,
there was everyday the intense excitement afforded
by the spelling-classes which occupied the last fifteen
minutes of school: the orderly filing forward; the
preservation of the straight line by marking with
one's toes the predetermined crack in the floor; the
calling out and subsequent spelling of the words; the
"going above," so fraught with anguish for one, with
triumph for another; the spectacular "leaving off at
the head" to begin again the next day upon the long
ascent; the presentation of *Merits* in blue or green,
red or purple.

In addition to these things there were enjoyments
and advantages furnished by the very fact that three
or four classes were housed, instructed, and examined
together in one room. When one's own lessons were
learned beyond any possibility of failure, it was not
difficult to obtain permission to sit still and listen to
whatever was being said and done in the recitation
seats or on the platform. This was a privilege es-

pecially esteemed by the younger children of each room, partly because it endowed one with a grown-up feeling, partly because its value was enhanced by the very quickness with which it was snatched away once the holder had proved unworthy. Thus, often long before one's own hour had come, one learned to pronounce, to spell, indeed to locate, Popocatapetl and Chimborazo, to know what manner of creature is the *llama,* and how Governor William Bradford stepped by chance into a grapevine trap in the Plymouth woods.

I feel personally greatly indebted to this custom and privilege because of a peculiarly vivid experience during my very first year in the lower school. My spelling-lesson learned and my one-column sums correctly added on my slate, I was allowed, late one morning, to look and to listen. A class in common fractions was engaged in doing some examples at the blackboard. Their numbers, so different from my own straight, one-columned sums, took on fascinating shapes, one above the other with strange signs between

$$\tfrac{1}{2} + \tfrac{3}{4} = \tfrac{2}{4} + \tfrac{3}{4} = \tfrac{5}{4} = 1\tfrac{1}{4}$$

To me these figures seemed not only beautiful but mysterious. It was one thing to copy numbers in a line; it was quite another to arrange them in these baffling relationships, numbers in pairs, numbers one above the other, numbers curiously increased at the close. About them lurked something hidden and inscrutable. Could it ever be that *I* should know the secrets of their orderly march across the blackboard? Unable to resist the temptation, I turned my own dull sums face down upon my desk and began to copy on the other side of my slate these bewildering symbols of something I knew not what.

It is impossible for me to describe or even to suggest the effect made upon me at six by those fractions upon that board and at length upon my own slate. There was a reverence in my contemplation of them which I can never forget. My later study of mathematics in any form, both at school and college, was inglorious in the extreme. I was, and remain, stupid beyond words. But that I have ever regarded the science with deference and awe I attribute to that morning in the village school when I first looked upon the beauty and the order of common fractions. Perhaps—who can tell?—in those minutes I glimpsed something of the harmony of mathematical law; perhaps, for once in my life, it was given me to fulfil Plato's injunction and ideal by looking upon arithmetic as a philosopher rather than as a shopkeeper.

CHAPTER IV

THE ACADEMY AND THE CLASSICAL TRADITION

(1)

THE academy in Blue Hill was founded in 1803 under the shadow and with the sanction of the Congregational Church; indeed, souls adhering to the Baptist faith were in the beginning of its long and honourable life charged for the development of their attendant and subservient minds a slightly higher rate of tuition. This arrangement was approved, if not in fact devised, by the Reverend Jonathan Fisher, its chief founder and most arduous support. From its start the school was strictly classical, both Latin and Greek and "the noble histories of these ancient peoples" being required of all students. The Reverend Mr. Fisher was saddened not a little "by the deplorable disregard to the Hebrew tongue," which he had hoped to teach the young men, but was obliged to content himself with the "careful instruction of the classical languages." He was at least spared the growing disregard of these as well which with the new century attacked his institution, substituting in their place the physical sciences and alas! as time has elapsed, the click of many typewriters in the so-called Commercial Course.

In the nineties, however, and the earliest years of the nineteen hundreds he would have remained at least relatively content, for the classics still held their honoured sway. Not all in the academy studied Greek, to be sure, but enough to demand that a preceptor be well-trained therein. Nor did all students study Latin, but enough to stamp the Classical Course as the course of the would-be scholar, the course of the gentleman and of the girl whose powers and whose educational ambitions were equal to those of her brother. No other, neither the Latin-Scientific nor the English Course, which was free of any language requirement, was in any sense its peer. The sons and the daughters of more practical tradesmen and farmers might, and often did, choose one or the other of these lesser curricula; but with such choice the tacit assumption was made and held by their teachers and themselves that their present intellectual capital was less commanding and their future attainments likely to be less distinguished. For thirty or forty years ago New England and, indeed, most of America still held the gifts of an ancient civilization bountiful, yea, necessary, to the adequate training and nourishment of her best minds.

It is easy and natural to account for the persistence of the classical tradition through almost three centuries on the grounds of heritage alone. It was inevitable that English colonists should bring from the mother country and establish in their new land an old and tried educational system. Thus we read with pleasure that Harvard College at its earliest was modelled in architecture and in learning alike after the home colleges at Cambridge within whose gracious quadrangles the leaders of Massachusetts Bay had been fostered. But what was neither so easy nor so natural was that the same tradition, at least in learning, should penetrate into the more remote parts of the country, even into the new West, and persist there in spite of every obstacle.

One likes to account for this survival and persistence not wholly on the grounds of heritage, to see in it again that synthesis of the hand and of the mind, which arose from the idealism, the freedom, the simplicity of American life and which has been earlier characterized in these pages. One likes, too, perhaps because it affords a humorous exercise in thinking, to reflect upon the fact that many of the classical writers were themselves countrymen and given to the labours of husbandry. How excellently well would they have fitted into new America! How perfectly, indeed, do they and their works exemplify the American synthesis! In the Massachusetts of 1630 Horace need not have made the burning subject of his prayers—*hoc erat in votis*—the possession of three acres and a cow! He might have had at least the acres for the taking! Vergil must needs have written a longer *Georgic* with fuller precepts for raising fruit on Maine hillsides. Cato, Varro, Hesiod—they knew the satisfaction of work with the hands and recognized with Pliny the Younger how wonderfully the mind is excited by the exercise of the body. *Mirum est ut animus agitatione motuque corporis excitetur.* Is there not perhaps some reason for assuming (a pleasant assumption at all events!) that a congeniality existed between the thoughts and the toil of primitive America and those of certain among the ancients, between the simplicity of their respective surroundings, and that this congeniality persisted so long as the simplicity was not destroyed?

Perhaps, too, the seafaring tradition did its part, on the Maine coast at least, to keep intact the classical. Not that sailors were taught or wanted to learn to read Cicero and Homer. Far from it! In their days and generations an undeniably more dramatic (not to say sensible) attitude was held toward training for a profession or for a business. Then education was variously defined; and not everyone was put as a matter of course through the schools. Yet the very fact that towns and villages were brought through their ships and their seamen into contact with other and older civilizations did much to foster and to preserve a respect for whatever those civilizations had offered to the world. Thus although my grandfather had been educated only in the hard school of the sea, although classics meant nothing to him, the familiar terms upon which he had ever been with Spanish and Italian ports formed a connecting link between the study of Latin and his grandchildren.

But explain as one will the survival of the classical tradition, base it upon the grounds of heritage, of synthesis, of congeniality, of connection through an industry seemingly divergent, the fact remains that twenty-five and thirty years ago the best-read and most thoughtful students of American academies and high schools were still reared on Latin and, to a less extent, on Greek. Nor, if my own experience can be used as evidence, were they conscious of any divorcement between their own daily concerns and those of the books they studied. The old age which Cicero portrayed, his ideals of patriotism and of friendship, were not foreign either to our experience or to our idealism. Vergil's old men and maidens, young men and children, had their counterparts, their tragedies and comedies, among us. Like Æneas in Dido's halls we might have said,

Sunt lacrimæ rerum et mentem mortalia tangunt.

The advice in Homer, which the aged and the experienced accorded the young and impulsive, the shipwrecks of Odysseus, the washing of clothes presumably on an Homeric Monday—these we unconsciously related to the life we knew. Even the high fields of Ithaca resembled the high Maine fields and pastures; its dark cliffs were not unlike our own; and there were many Eugénie de Guérins who imagined themselves Nausicaa as they spread the family linen on the summer grass.

The classics, moreover, performed for the New

England adolescent a spiritual service which has been too little recognized and recorded. In the barrenness of our Puritan heritage, where right was right and wrong was wrong, where goodness was to be embraced because it was dutiful and desirable and where village opinion united with Heaven and the Scriptures in condemning as abhorrent, shortcomings which were often the result only of misdirected good, the classics struck sudden and refreshing wells of water. We became now and then conscious that the good might be identical with the beautiful, the orderly, the harmonious, that the bad was to be condemned not alone because it was bad but rather because it was ugly, confusing, and out of tune. Most stupendous of all, we discovered that even physical loveliness might be looked upon (discreetly, of course) as a gift from Heaven instead of being regarded as a possible, yea, *likely* avenue to the blackest of sins. Thus the stern morals and ethics even of our day were transcended by Vergil and by Homer, and pity was allowed her alleviating ministrations. In our own case at least, since our spiritual lot in the broadening thought of the world was to be kinder than that of our forebears, this transcendence did not cease with adolescence or with our years at the village academy.

(2)

In its main lines the education afforded us at the academy was in no way at variance with that of the village school; indeed, the methods employed in our instruction were very much the same. Here, too, there were no extras, no frills. Music, art, manual training, domestic science,—these were unknown. There was, in the first place, no money for them; in the second, had there been means, their ultimate value would have been seriously questioned. Our lessons were prescribed; we learned and recited them; and although, now that we were older, there were rarely tears over failures and more often recalcitrants who rebelled against higher learning, for the most part we continued as docile and as obedient to authority as we had been in our earlier years.

Those who elected the Classical Course studied Latin for four years, Greek for three, and history, mathematics, and English throughout; those in the Latin-Scientific substituted sciences for Greek and during their last two years French for history; those in the English course had no languages at all and in their place such makeshifts as Commercial and Physical Geography, Civics, and a sturdy review of Arithmetic. The academy was badly equipped for sciences, a few bottles, test-tubes, and instruments in a tiny room supplementing the meticulous, if elementary, study of scientific theory. In the nineties and early nineteen hundreds the interest of teachers and of parents alike was centred in the Classical or College Preparatory Course. Now inevitably that has changed, not because fewer students attend college (for each September their widening ranks are startling to the thoughtful observer) but because fewer colleges demand a thorough grounding in classics.

Blue Hill Academy in the nineties recognized, cherished, and strove to maintain a high and honourable tradition. Perhaps, as in the church, there lingered about her brick walls and white portico something of the indomitable spirit of the Reverend Jonathan Fisher, who, it may be recalled, was master of many tongues and propounded his texts Sunday by Sunday in Hebrew or in Greek. She was proud of the preceptors who, coming from wider fields to Blue Hill, had after a varying period of years left for larger destinies. She could point among these to judges and justices, professors of colleges, members of foreign embassies. In 1903 when she held her centennial there were brilliant robes and hoods worn by her teachers and her graduates alike in the academic procession which wound through the June fields to her doorway.

The teachers of my own day continued to do honour to her history. They were without an exception graduates of fine institutions, men and women of cultivation and background. They prepared us well for college and better for life and thought. Unrelenting, perhaps pedantic, as they were in their teaching, they taught us to work at a task until we had finished it, distasteful as it might be; and they were none too lavish of their assistance. The more I deal with the products of modern educational systems, the longer I strive to instruct the output of the experimental school with its insistence upon a large measure of "self-discipline," the deeper the gratitude I accord my own teachers of thirty years ago. Self-discipline in the classical schools of the nineties, as of the years preceding, was interpreted to mean the discipline possible by the self only after the self had been *disciplined* by outward as well as by inward forces. To me, at least, this seems an eminently reasonable definition.

For the most part our excitements, and they were many and varied, were centred within and rose from the affairs of school. We had a dramatic society which enacted scenes from Shakespeare, with home-made costumes on an improvised Elizabethan stage. These after hours of practice we presented before our parents, who paid ten cents each for the privilege or the pain of seeing an inarticulate son do Hamlet's soliloquy or a plain daughter forget herself as Lady Macbeth. We fostered among a select and secret few the literary instinct, meeting weekly after school with an adored teacher. Here, after repeated urgings and encouragement, we read our own bad verse, modelled upon the sing-song rhythms of Alice and Phœbe Cary, and worse prose inspired by the fine stories of Sarah Orne Jewett, then at the height of her fame and much admired by our leader.

Perhaps chief among our most pleasurable concerns was a debating club, known as the Webster-Hayne Society. Throughout the academy and even throughout the village the loyalty accorded to this organization was intense. Debates were held once a fortnight between opposing teams of two each; and since it was the aim of the club to be inclusive rather than selective in the choice of its speakers, opportunity was widespread for this legitimate means of self-expression. Our subjects were many and varied, and it was an unalterable rule that we should *draw* both for them and for the side we were to support. Thus it was conceivable that I, who would have liked to defend the heroism of the American Indian, or the pre-eminence of sailing vessels over steamships, might be compelled to denounce the Monroe Doctrine or the Assassination of Julius Cæsar. The preceptor of my day, who was responsible for this rule as well as for the list of suggested subjects, maintained that by this method of assignment we were trained in the necessary virtue of adaptability; and my father, who was for years a patron of the society, entirely agreed with him.

We usually wrote our arguments and then committed them to memory, although gifted ones among us might prefer to speak "off-hand." The rebuttal which followed the debate proper always called for some spontaneous denouncing of our rivals, which, in the heat of the controversy, we found not too difficult in spite of a large and interested audience. A letter of commendation from my father, written from Augusta a few days following my spirited denunciation of Napoleon as a monster to civilization, is one of my treasured possessions as is also a notebook which lists our subjects of one winter term:

Resolved, that the American Indian was, on the whole, an heroic rather than a dastardly figure in history.

Resolved, that the system of taxation under the Roman Empire was unjust to the provinces.

Resolved, that the study of Greek is valuable to the student in Blue Hill Academy.

Resolved, that the Annexation of Texas was unjustifiable.

Resolved, that the rural life of Maine affords advantages above that of the urban.

Resolved, that "Ivanhoe" is a greater and a more interesting novel than "The Last of the Mohicans."

Even the love affairs of the academy were promoted and fostered by interests intellectual as well as social. Some of them might almost be said to have been *classically* conducted. What, indeed, could be more seemingly innocent and yet more provocative of youthful passion than hours spent together over Dido, abandoned, heart-sick and desperate? The prepositions governing the dative might credibly assume major proportions were one assisted through the intricacies of the sentences based upon them by the recipient of one's admiration and ardour. I well remember with what enhanced pleasure I regarded, on my fifteenth birthday, the romantic gift of a pair of gloves because of the presentation message in careful Latin concealed in one of the thumbs. The staid framers of the Latin Grammar which we used in the academy were doubtless innocent of including

therein any incitements to susceptive or impression-
able hearts. Yet who among us was so prudent or so
dull as not to seize gratefully upon appropriate sentences or verses in the appendix of selections for
translation, placed at the end of the book and ready
for many an inarticulate pen. What so reasonable or
so helpful as to emulate Pliny to Calpurnia.

> It is impossible to say how much I miss you.
> *Incredible est, quanto desiderio tui tenear.*

or

Propertius to Cynthia:

How many gifts did I give her or how many songs did I
　sing her!
Nevertheless she, that iron creature, never once said "I
　love you."

Munera quanta dedi vel qualia carmina feci!
illa tamen numquam ferrea dixit "Amo."

CHAPTER V

COLLEGE LIFE AT THE BEGINNING OF
THE NEW CENTURY

MY older sister and I chose our colleges while we were still in our early years at the academy. Her choice was Wellesley, and she was influenced in making it by the fact that we had relatives in Boston. Mine was Brown University, my favourite teacher having been trained there. My parents were inclined to encourage my selection largely on account of the Dean of Women at Brown, then Anne Crosby Emery, formerly of Ellsworth and a friend of my father. Miss Emery, now Mrs. Francis Greenleaf Allinson of Providence and wife of the late eminent scholar and professor of Greek at Brown, was herself a classicist of repute. She has since those years become widely known for her books and essays on classical subjects.

Circumstances, however, did not favour our dreams. My father, who was known to be intensely loyal to Maine, became one of a group formed for the purpose of promoting state institutions. Consistency demanded that, since he had children of college age, he support as well as promote. Moreover, it was actively borne in upon us all that two might be sent to college within the state for the cost of one outside her borders and that the family treasury, never overly large, would be taxed to its utmost with seven to be educated. Reared upon the principle as well as the necessity of co-operation, my sister and I, without too much regret, relinquished our desires and prepared to enter the University of Maine in the fall of 1904.

My father had selected the University in preference to either of the two colleges in the state which admitted women. He was influenced partly by the fact that it was numbered among the institutions he was pledged to support, partly by his regard for its teaching staff, which he had carefully inquired into. He was impressed also by the knowledge not only that we should be among the first women entering the University but also that we should be taught with men, who in numbers at least would far eclipse us. Twenty-five years ago, incredible as it may seem today, there was drama in the contemplation of competition between the sexes! Accordingly in September of 1904, after three nerve-racking days of writing entrance examinations at the University, my sister and I were admitted, and watched, not without pleasure and excitement, our gratified parents depart for home.

The Maine colleges, with the sole exception of Bowdoin, which has ever been more heterogeneous, "extra-state," and urbane in its social and, to a large extent, in its intellectual aspects, have always been relatively simple, not to say *provincial* institutions. I use the second adjective advisedly and in its best sense, meaning thereby not the want of culture and polish of the capital, but rather the hardy and rural character conferred upon them by the background of the great majority of their students. Maine is, comparatively, not a wealthy state. The larger number of her people are neither urban nor suburban but rural, if the word be used to include those living in the country towns and villages, which far outnumber her cities. Of the five hundred students who constituted the University of Maine during my four years there, ninety per cent were from the state and of that ninety per cent the vast majority came from country places. One has but to be cursorily acquainted with, for instance, the colleges and universities of Massachusetts to recognize the distinct difference between their attitude and atmosphere and the attitude and atmosphere of the Maine institutions. And although twenty-five years have wrought changes on Maine campuses as elsewhere, the distinction remains much the same today.

Needless to say, there was little money among us in 1904, but there were better things than money. With few exceptions we came from homes which were making sacrifices for us, and a decent sense of obligation demanded that we be not lethargic toward our advantages. Many if not most of the young men (there were but twenty-one women at the time of my entrance) were partly self-supporting either by work in summer or during their college course. Of the eighteen girls in the one dormitory for women all came from good Maine families, several from outstanding ones. Not one of the eighteen had a monthly allowance of over five dollars; in fact, that sum was held to be extremely generous. An invitation to a select society, which asked an equal amount as an initiation fee, occasioned long and detailed letters to and from home on so weighty a matter, so monstrous a tax on the family exchequer, since the advantages to be obtained therefrom could be honestly designated as neither intellectual nor moral.

As I look about upon the girls of the college with which I am now associated, I indulge in delighted, not to say humorous, retrospect upon the wardrobes which my sister and I in one trunk transported to our Alma Mater. These had been prepared with no little foresight and care by my mother and the village seamstress, a practical if not versatile woman with a distinct talent for "making over." We, I may say at the outset, were completely satisfied, indeed somewhat dazed, by the character and the extent of our new clothes. We had each one party dress, my sister's a white swiss muslin, mine a dark blue voile sprigged with white and entrancingly fashioned with the new scalloped shoulder, made of tucked white organdie and beaded with black velvet. We had each a woollen dress for afternoons and Sundays, hers of dark red serge, mine of brown. Mine, however, to compensate for its dulness of colour, was equipped with a wide, bertha-like collar of heavy white lace, detachable at will. My father, who shared with me an indescribable admiration for this, called it a "tidy." Blue sailor-suits for every day; kimonos of bright outing flannels; two cotton dresses and three shirt-waists each (an exorbitant supply!); extra skirts of blue serge; a new winter coat apiece which had been bought by mail order from Bangor after many had been sent down "on approval"; two pairs of shoes, high for common, low for best; and a truly extravagant supply of underwear, especially of starched petticoats—all these things made my sister and me the envy of other households than our own!

The most stupendous innovations demand a paragraph by themselves. These were our gymnasium suits. They had been ordered by the authorities of the University and consented to by my father with no little misgiving but with the assurance that, since they were required, *he* was in no way responsible. The very full and entirely decorous bloomers were constructed by the seamstress after a careful and none too approving laying on of patterns. The accompanying blue flannel blouses, since they were made with long sleeves, were a source of some reassurance to my mother, who recognized that they could with decency be worn with skirts and thus constitute other costumes. My mother was also somewhat reassured by the discovery that, if we stood perfectly still, the bloomers, which had been such a source of embarrassment to both her and the seamstress, resembled a full and reasonably long skirt; and my sister and I took good care not to suggest the improbability of standing still long in a gymnasium! To us both these suits represented not only an exciting divorcement from the life we knew but also our entrance into an untried field of endeavour; and we arrayed ourselves repeatedly behind the closed door of our room.

I can only assure my readers (and many of my own generation will need no assurance) that the appearance of my sister and me, daily, on Sunday, and at evening social events, was in every way equal to that of our associates. Silk dresses were virtually unknown among us, and there was not a pair of silk stockings nor yet of distinctly evening shoes in the dormitory. One girl, whose father was a foreign sea-captain of one of the few remaining sailing-ships in the European trade, was the possessor of a Chinese wrap which could be used for negligee or for evening wear; but since there was only one of its kind among us, we looked upon it with curiosity rather than with envy.

Needless to say, life was simple, perhaps even somewhat serious, though never overly so. In common with the other five freshman girls we learned to dance, being taught the waltz, two-step, and more complicated schottische by our older contemporaries. Probably we danced badly (I speak more particularly of my own poor progress) but we managed to qualify for the evening parties which were held not too frequently at one or another fraternity house and at stated intervals in the college gymnasium. We learned tennis also, and in the winter snowshoeing was deservedly popular on the long white reaches of the Stillwater and the Penobscot.

At the risk of being termed pedantic, I must admit that we enjoyed our studies. The time and the situation alike gave no place in our dormitory for the girl who comes to college for experience, or for social prestige, or for want of something better to do, or for the perpetuation of a family tradition. We were all there for business, and we knew it. Twenty-five and thirty years ago families still held days of reckoning; and these in Maine families of small cash resources were apt to be serious affairs. Since as a matter of course we all studied Latin, we prepared our Livy and Horace in a group, the least ardent holding the dictionary, the best translator held in reserve for the final polishing. Since only one of the seven freshman girls was enlisted with me in Greek (for even then the tide was turning!) we did our Homer, Xenophon, and certain of the tragedies together through many a stirring hour for two years.

My sister decided to specialize in Latin and in mathematics. I, in contrast to her, was the discouragement of at least six instructors in algebra, solid geometry, and trigonometry, who handed me about among themselves in the forlorn hope that one among them might find some remedy for my inexplicable and monstrous stupidity. Unlike the lady in Barrie's *Quality Street* the University did not hold

algebra and its concomitant evils "unladylike subjects." Women as well as men were required to complete a year of mathematics, no matter the cost, which
for me was heavy in spite of my sister's exasperated
assistance. My own choice of subjects was Greek and,
to my father's intense pleasure, history. The University was especially strong in both departments. My
Greek class, which was held every afternoon at two
o'clock, was the most momentous hour of my day.
The professor, who with Hesiod exemplified the
classical synthesis of literature and farming, came
from his barns and his fields to his class-room; and
he often willingly stayed an extra hour or longer to
introduce us to Theocritus or Aristophanes or to read
with us again in new understanding the immortal
hexameters of Homer.

Those afternoons, stirring with new perceptions
and wide with new-old visions, I can never forget.
Because of them I look with unfeigned pity upon the
college freshmen of today who regard Greek as dead
and "useless" and who are encouraged in this base-
less and unfledged opinion by lenient or utilitarian
parents. For the relinquishment of Homer alone
offers no substitute. Surely he himself is Plato's
ideal, in spite of Plato's banishment of him from the
Perfect State. He is the "spectator of all time and
existence"; and his limitless wisdom in all things
must perforce cultivate to some degree even the most
thoughtless minds. The rhythm of his lines, now
plunging with the "surge and thunder" of his own

unharvested sea, now flowing with the music of his own rivers, Ægyptus and Selleëis, Oceanus, Xanthos, and Parthenios, has nowhere an equal. In its harmony lies hidden the mystical key to many a world of beauty, of contemplation, of knowledge transcendent. And as for those more tangible graces which the children of this world, ever more numerous than the "children of Light," rightly value, what literature has more of these than the Homeric poems? There is assuredly no good quality lacking in them. Courage, manliness, pity, humour, justice, reverence for old age and for the home,—all these are there, and all these were ours in those short winter afternoons in our tower room of Wingate Hall. Immortal images, too, we carried away as we crunched homeward across the early-lighted snow. Odysseus as a child choosing some apple trees "for his very own"; the Trojan women working at their looms; the Phæacian barks that needed no help of the oar; Glaucus and Sarpedon with the shining shields of Lycia behind them; Circe casting the golden shuttle through her loom of gold; Homeric kine "with trailing feet and shambling gait"; the trusty Eurycleia lighting the young Telemachus to his chamber high up in the fair court. What wonder that on many an afternoon we lingered over our Greek until "the sun had sunk and all the ways were darkened"?

Equally fortunate was I in my history professor, who was then the only woman of a ranking position on the faculty. She had been trained for her doctorate under no less an historian than Professor Edward Cheyney of the University of Pennsylvania, and her teaching was admirable in the extreme. Under her thorough and careful demands I learned to read more searchingly than I had ever read before, until the pain of my bewildered mind began to give way before the relief afforded by steady mental exercise, thoughtfully, if sternly, administered.

English composition was required of us all for the first year, and I took always great delight therein. Our ideals and models were selected for us from such sound and incontestable sources as the nineteenth century giants: Hazlitt, Lamb, De Quincey, Macaulay, and Stevenson. The "moderns" of the first decade of the present century were looked upon rather sceptically by the great majority of English instructors everywhere in so far as their worth for purposes of emulation was concerned.

I had, however, during my first year in college a teacher to whom I shall always be grateful. The University authorities not agreeing with my estimate, he tarried among us but a short season. He was, I presume, a young radical of his day; he had, I know, little use for the conventions of teaching. Under his guidance, although we did not forsake the old and the tried, we took daring excursions into more modern fields both in reading and in literary endeavour. We read George Meredith and Thomas Hardy (still sharply under fire for *Jude the Obscure* which even our instructor did not venture to recommend) as well as the writers most in evidence in our own country, Alice Brown, F. Hopkinson Smith, Sarah Orne Jewett, and, most baffling of all, Mr. Henry James. In writing we did very much as we liked, constructing plays, indulging in poems, sometimes even of the Walt Whitman variety, or in descriptions modelled perhaps on Lafcadio Hearn. I learned from this teacher the first principles and practices of criticism; moreover, he lodged firmly in my mind the truth that one can conceivably think well of something which he personally does not like. This was borne in upon me by his good-humoured tolerance of my adolescent admiration for Mr. Henry van Dyke, then at the height of his somewhat circumscribed fame.

Alas! Emanicipated perhaps from morals as well as from true scholastic principles, our instructor fell before his superiors in rank and position. It was rumoured that he was intoxicated over many a week-end. Certain it was that he consistently absented himself, much to our grief, from his Monday classes. But since another species of intoxication was his and ours on Wednesdays and Fridays—an intoxication disseminated by few teachers in few institutions!—I have never ceased to regret that ethics, triumphing as often in matters terrestrial over genius, resulted in his hasty dismissal.

The remaining three years broadened and deepened our progress in the studies of our choice as well as provided new ones, required or elective. In the sciences, which were well taught but, fortunately for me, not required beyond one basic year, I was very much at sea, detesting both laboratory and microscope. Of psychology I had, unfortunately, nothing; indeed, almost nothing was taught, in Maine at least, during the first decade of the century. Nor might I at that time traverse at any length into the far-reaching and Hesperidean fields of philosophy, although Plato's *Phædo* and *Symposium* and certain books of the *Republic* became even then spiritual ministrations, *per omnia in sæcula sæculorum*. As for "education," we knew it only as a necessity or an enjoyment, not as a professional subject to be taught and learned. I remember that in my last year the University imported such an "educator," who instructed prospective teachers in the development of the embryo as well as in the principles of Froebel, Rousseau and Pestalozzi concerning the mental development of the child once he was born. It was difficult, I recall, to take his classes seriously as we took Greek, mathematics, history, or English.

Besides the discipline of the class-room and of prescribed study there was time in the first decade of the century for excursions into reading of one's own. College life was less complicated and, above all, less noisy. Even in 1908 and 1909 the horn of an automobile in Maine rarely disturbed one. We walked more, talked and thought more than the average students of today, even although our talk and our thought (not to mention our walk!) were far less emancipated. I recall long hours in the library spent in desultory reading. Stephen Crane's *The Red Badge of Courage*, Wilkie Collins' *Moonstone* and *The Woman in White*, A. Conan Doyle's *The White Company*, Trollope's *Barchester Towers*—I remember waking from these to find the clock past the hour for dinner or for a class. Perhaps in their way, in the pleasure and excitement they afforded, they counted for as much as the more intellectual excitement engendered by the robust and new philosophy of *Sartor Resartus*, also a college discovery of my own.

When I graduated in 1909, having remained out a year for experience in teaching, I suppose I was as insufficiently trained as are most college graduates from most institutions in any given year at any given period. The chief claim which I can make for my fitness for life and living was that I, like many at least of my contemporaries, left with certain deep-rooted enthusiasms, desires, and ideals: an enthusiasm for thought and for study; a desire for knowledge for its own sake because of the sheer fun in it; a consciousness of certain *objective* values which, although perhaps dimly defined and possibly sentimental, were nevertheless secure. These intellectual and spiritual possessions, which, I take it, every college and university desires above all others to give its graduates, had not been lost to me or rendered difficult of attainment through the thousand conflicting interests which the hurrying, unstable society of most cam-

puses makes inevitable today. That this was true as it
cannot be true of the college life in which I now live
was simply my good fortune—one of the amenities
of a simpler environment and of a simpler age, which
doubtless lacked quite as much as it possessed.

CHAPTER VI

THE DISTRICT SCHOOL

THERE has surely been an overproduction of sentimentalism, both spoken and written, concerning the country or district school—that unique American institution which forty or even thirty years ago was indispensable to the educational system of every state. Presidents have found an easier way to the White House if they could supply their campaign managers and orators with details of its peculiar advantages in the building of their characters. In the lauding of its service as a handmaiden to Democracy, of its barefoot boys, McGuffey Readers, and initialled desks, of its idyllic sylvan surroundings and the womanly and manly virtues which it supposedly engendered and nurtured, many of its liabilities have been generously overlooked.

These more unlyrical features—its draughts, its airtight stove, common water-pail and long-handled dipper, its ill-paid, untrained teachers and crowded curriculum—have in the steady march of progress caused its almost complete annihilation. Even in the most isolated sections districts have become consolidated, superintendents placed in charge, modern buildings erected with sanitary drinking fountains and central heat, and state certificates required of all teachers. School busses now furrow their way through rocky Maine roads as over the mountainous trails of Wyoming; and children clamber into them with ten cents in their pockets for a morning glass of milk with a graham cracker and a well-planned hot luncheon served from the school kitchen. School nurses now see to it that epidemics are halted, that teeth are properly brushed, and that more frequent baths are encouraged if not actually administered beneath the new showers.

Thus the country school is rapidly becoming a thing of the past, dead as are free church suppers, double-seated pungs, and top buggies. Yet its fruits were many, in Maine as elsewhere. Surely the mental agility which it required and developed in its teachers was deserving of commendation as well as the manual effectiveness which it often exacted from them. And when all its debits and credits are duly arranged, the latter outweigh the former in at least one respect —because of the humour which a period of teaching therein was sure to afford a reasonably open mind.

I began my twenty-five years' experience as a teacher at the age of nineteen in a district school on the coast of Maine. It was in the spring of 1906 while I was still a student at college. In those years it was quite the normal thing for one to leave his studies to acquire not only experience in his future profession but a little money as well. Family fortunes at the time being none too prosperous and my father, moreover, feeling with some justice that I might well test my own resources in more practical ways than study, I was assigned, largely through his influence, as teacher for the spring term of a somewhat undesirable school. This was situated in a fishing community, or more properly speaking, settlement some twelve miles distant from Blue Hill.

My father himself drove me to my destination early on a cold, raw, comfortless morning in April. Never so long as I live shall I forget the fear, inadequacy, and indecision which seemingly lay, with my scanty and hurried breakfast, in the very pit of my stomach during those miles through mud and rain. The school was reputed to be a "hard" one; and my father was not chary with injunctions and advice. I not only easily gathered that it was entirely up to me whether I fought my way through or went down in ignominious defeat; I *knew*, knowing my father, that only the first course was possible.

He deposited me with all my belongings (for no family had as yet offered hospitality to the new teacher) before the school-house door at precisely quarter to nine. It seemed to me I had never seen so many children of all ages and sizes as the number which stood about in an appraising circle as I stepped from the muddy carriage. My father said good-bye, pressing as he did so an unwieldy package into my hand with a murmured command not to be slow in using it when necessary. It proved to be a razor strop and, if I must speak truthfully, a veritable godsend.

The school-house stood upon a rocky ledge but a short distance from the sea. As I entered it that first morning, I felt and saw the salt mist and fog, driven by the east wind, precede me into its drab and ugly interior. The pupils numbered forty-nine, and they ranged in ages and sizes from boys of eighteen to little girls of four and five. On that dreadful first day I could not be consoled by the knowledge that once the weather and sea improved for coast seafaring of various sorts, the oldest and most ominous of my male population would leave me in comparative peace.

Dictates both of the Scriptures and of enlightened educational principles enjoin a rule of love rather than one of force. Nevertheless, district schools are not recorded in the New Testament; and it is at least questionable whether the most mild and pacific of educators ever attempted to govern one of the worst variety. A rule of love on that April morning in the year 1906 would have failed me utterly. Desperate situations entail desperate remedies. Long before my father and his horse were halfway home, I found myself threatened with my own exit by way of the window; and I turned to my razor strop with a furious gratitude!

Nowhere than in such a school as my first is better evidenced the respectful fear engendered by any exhibition of the lack of it. The threats of gaunt young sailors and fishermen, before any one of whom I should have been utterly powerless, vanished into air before my own pretence of bravery. It was a poor enough pretence, framed by necessity and by very normal rage; but it worked. From those few minutes onwards, although my knees were failing me throughout the day, discipline through ten long weeks was never again a major problem.

My knees had yet another reason to fail me before that interminable day came to an end at four o'clock. In the hurry of so early a departure from home the lunch with which my mother had generously provided me had somehow been overlooked and omitted from my baggage. At twelve o'clock, while dinner-pails and boxes were opened by my hungry pupils, my own bags failed to reveal anything edible except one large cucumber pickle, packed separately by itself in a brown paper bag. I was too much an object of awe as I sat at my desk for any of my charges to offer me refreshment if, indeed, my plight were recognized, as it probably was not. I remember the monstrous depths of self-pity in which I ate my cucumber. The vitamins, which even then it must have contained, were insufficient to replenish my waning energy; and I was in a sorry state when at supper time a none too eager housewife grudgingly offered me bed and board at three dollars per week from my salary of ten.

The eleven weeks in that country school were—I state this stupendous truth with no reservations, silly as it may sound—the most valuable weeks of my life. With twenty-nine separate classes to be taught daily, with forty-nine children not only to be disciplined but to be considered with decent regard to each as an individual, with a refractory stove to tend on cold and wet April mornings and a school-room to sweep, with problems in compound proportion to be wept over until solved every night and innumerable papers to correct, with a score of none too intelligent parents to be mollified and enlisted—with all these things and many more, one's own problems, one's adolescent vanities, heart-burnings, and self-pity were necessarily pushed into so remote a background as to be completely lost to view. At just the time when I most needed such an experience, I lost sight of my importunate, clamouring self—a salutary loss, indeed.

Resources which I never knew I possessed came to my aid to become especially useful as the spring advanced. Many of the young men, whose submission had resulted in their adherence, went to sea on coasting-vessels or on summer yachts; but as the fishing increased, their places were soon filled. Mothers could and must be utilized in the cleaning and packing of fish; and babies must be cared for by someone. By the middle of May there was hardly a morning without its supply of infants, ranging from six months to two years. These constituted my major problem. They could not be allowed to crawl about the school-room nor could they be held by older brothers and sisters intent upon square root and the French and Indian Wars. They must be rendered at least relatively quiet if school were to be school in any honest sense of the word.

Cautiously trained instructors of our modern nursery schools will be rightly incensed at the only ways and means open to me in such an exigency as this. The village cooper came to my rescue with four large and clean barrels, which I placed one in each corner. Each would decently accommodate four small babies during their morning naps or secure two or three of more advanced age against creeping about on the floor. If worse came to worst, as it often did, some sugar tied in a bit of cotton cloth proved an indispensable solace, although it was utilized only *in extremis*. Those barrels proved the salvation not only of my school but of my own sanity. On late May mornings, when the sun lay warm on the rocky ledges and wild pear trees hung their frail blossoms over the log fences, I taught on, relatively undisturbed from eight drowsy babies within their secure enclosures!

In September, for I had decided to teach yet another year before returning to college, I was "called up higher," given a better school in a slightly larger locality. Here, although babies were kept at home, I was faced with an epidemic of whooping-cough. The young of the entire community being stricken, it was quite sensibly decided that the school-house was as safe a place of detention as any other. There is no mother who does not understand the baneful significance of whooping-cough contracted in the late summer or autumn! Whooping and strangling with their unpleasant concomitants continued during the winter term as well and lingered, or returned, to make memorable the ten weeks of the spring. Nor were matters improved by an especially severe winter. In the morning I broke the ice in my pitcher to wash my face and hands in an icy room and hurried early through the snow to coax a temperamental stove with wood which my older boys and I had cut from a nearby pasture.

I am sure my pupils in these schools learned little. It was I who was educated. Considering the manifold blessings I received from this versatile apprenticeship to the teaching profession, I am incapable of looking with unqualified favour upon its surrender in the wake of progress to easier, less sturdy ways. Doubtless my reaction is, as "reactions" usually are, sentimental and valueless rather than critical and wise. Yet I cannot be forgetful of the intellectual and social capital with which I returned to college after four terms of teaching a district school: the power of holding my own mind to a given task; the ability for quick decision; the recognition of my own mental defects and of possible mental assets; the clearer knowledge of what I wanted to do in the world; and, last but not least, an awakened and enlarged sense of humour. So much cause have I, indeed, to bless the country school for these as well as other gifts that I look with eager confidence upon the rare college instructor who can state that in her formative years she taught even one term of an ungraded rural school in any relatively untrammelled wilderness!

But a new world was soon to hurtle about the battered doors even of such a remote institution as this. With the outbreak of the Great War, after five years of teaching in more up-to-date schools, I began my graduate study. When I had done and entered upon college teaching, I found, like all others of my age and generation, a new civilization in which to live and work, converting whatever had been of value throughout a relatively stable past into capital for a new and unstable present.

EPILOGUE

I CANNOT claim with the Duchess of Newcastle that I have intended my book to "divulge the truth" rather than to "delight the reader" or to "please his fancy." Unlike her who wished after-ages not to forget her illustrious lineage, I have had no such momentous truths to divulge; and I have frankly hoped that these less pretentious chronicles may serve, first of all, to amuse and to entertain their chance readers. That they are, however, true and accurate few of my own generation and none of my own environment will question.

My book claims no such weighty possession as a thesis unless, perhaps, the term may be applied to the idea of experience as its own end and goal. It pretends to be nothing except the noting of those circumstances and events, those attendant thoughts and impressions, which form the mind and the spirit of an age or of a period. It pretends to do nothing except to record a certain process of that brain-building by which we are, each one of us, what we are.

Yet before it comes to a conclusion, perhaps too long deferred, I would correct a statement and an impression of an early page which I have seen in the gradual unfolding of these chapters to be manifestly untrue. I said, and perhaps believed, at the beginning that most of the middle-aged among us were by early training, environment, and education unprepared for the New World in which we must live. I see now that the best of us have had instead an invincible preparation.

To have been reared in relative simplicity in an age less homogeneous than the present, less monotonous in its freedom from machinery; to have belonged to a people rather than to a nation; to have been encouraged, through the wholesome principle of co-operation, in identity but discouraged in "individualism"; to have inherited as a birthright long hours for reading and for thought in a world less encumbered by books of every sort and less frantic with half-fledged ideas; to have spent a relatively free and untrammelled childhood and adolescence before the advent of moving and talking pictures and before the tortuous organization of one's social life and activities; to have known the quiet of village, even of city streets; to have lived closer to traditions with their manifold and engrossing excitements; to have known intimately or through books and persons the new life of a still-existing frontier, parts of a soil and a country yet to be made by character and enterprise—these are gifts not lightly to be set aside.

Nor was the Puritanism which we knew, less tenacious though it had become in our day, without its beneficent influences also. For in that it gave us a sense of, yea, a faith in immutable values, enduring, permanent, secure in their changelessness, it was to become as the shadow of a great rock in a weary land. Renovation and adaptation in the conception of truths may be salutary and necessary; but faith in the existence of the truths themselves—truths objective and eternal, not dependent for their existence upon one's rejection or upon one's adherence, truths changeless as the Universals of Plato, indeed, identical with them—such faith is indispensable to the rich and constructive minds of any people or of any age, a pillar of fire by night and of cloud by day. With it one is surely armour-proof against confusion or seeming instability; with it any man, if he will, may "set his own house in order."

As to our education we were singularly blessed. Standing on the threshold of the new and not untouched by its influences, we were yet reared and disciplined upon the old foundations. Ours was perhaps the last of many generations who will have studied the classics as a matter of course and received to the fullest extent their illimitable and gracious effects. We were also perhaps the last to participate in rather than to look back upon that peculiarly American synthesis of the hand and the mind, to recite Greek and Latin hexameters while we drove cows to pasture or helped, like Nausicaa, to spread the Monday's washing in the field.

Surely the lines fell unto us in pleasant places, places meet to prepare us for the Newest of worlds. That we missed much of all which the New Age possesses, of all which will doubtless prove its own goodly heritage to those of its generation—this is incontestable. But the wise among us will seize upon whatsoever things are here and now of good report because of their larger honesty and justice, cultivating meanwhile from the gifts tendered especially unto ourselves a merry relinquishment as well as a larger understanding.